What people are saying about …

THE TOP TEN LEADERSHIP COMMANDMENTS

"I highly recommend you read this fresh look at leadership lessons from the life of Moses that set him apart as one of the greatest leaders in all of history. This hero of the Bible was used by God to deliver a nation. Learn how a reluctant leader survived and succeeded in one of history's greatest leadership challenges: taking his people from bondage in Egypt to the door of the Promised Land. Not just classroom theory, these chapters are filled with practical applications for twenty-first-century leaders based on the story of Moses applied to the decades of leadership experienced by Dr. Finzel."

Coach Bill McCartney, founder and chairman
of the board of Promise Keepers

"Burnout. Social media exhaustion. Personal life meltdowns. Ego drunkenness. There are countless pitfalls surrounding modern leadership. This book shows you how to face them, avoid them, and ultimately beat them with a God who wants healthy, whole leaders."

Jon Acuff, Wall Street Journal best-selling
author of *Quitter: Closing the Gap between
Your Day Job & Your Dream Job*

"This book is for every leader. Whether successful or struggling, we all need this! Hans Finzel has articulated for us the rules of the road for effectiveness. The thing I love about Hans and his writing is that it is forged out of years of experience and a deep understanding of the way kingdom leaders need to live and lead."

Joe Stowell, president of Cornerstone University

"Whenever my friend Hans Finzel writes or speaks about leadership, he has my full attention. His insights are compelling because they are grounded in truth, tested by experience, and on full display in and through his life and ministry."

Dr. Crawford W. Loritts, Jr., author, speaker, radio host, and senior pastor of Fellowship Bible Church in Roswell, GA

"There is no lack of books on leadership, many of which seem to come out of an 'ivory tower' of theory. However, Hans Finzel writes from practical experience filtered through biblical truths and guidelines. *The Top Ten Leadership Commandments* is based on what we learn from the life and leadership challenges of Moses but reflects Finzel's years of mission leadership and training leaders. It is insightful and applicable to any leadership role, but especially for those called to lead spiritual tasks in church and mission."

Jerry Rankin, president emeritus of International Mission Board, SBC

"Each commandment both warns and advises a leader who has *ears to hear*. Commandments 4 and 5 are worth the price of the book. Hans' methodology—reflecting on Moses' experience, intermingled with experiences from his own life—powerfully teaches these leadership lessons. Hans's desire, and one of the major purposes of this book, is that Moses' leadership prayer may be realized in your leadership (Ps. 90:12, 17—effective leadership and resulting legacy). Leaders with *leadership ears to hear* will be amply rewarded by reading this book-long encouragement to continue leading and finish well. Hans has modeled and is modeling for us what he teaches in these Ten Commandments."

"In a crowded field, this book stands out. Clear. Concise. Humble. Visionary. Biblical. It's exactly what a leader needs to keep stepping back into the ring to face the challenges of leadership today."

"Hans Finzel has had the habit of cheering me on in my journey as a developing leader. He always takes the time as one of our trustees to encourage me and affirm my efforts at leadership. Every book he publishes adds to his deposits in my life. *The Top Ten Leadership Commandments* transparently articulates lessons learned in the crucible of laying your life down in the service of others. Reading the book not only made Moses come alive but added fuel to my heart's fire to serve as an effective leader of God's people."

THE TOP TEN
LEADERSHIP
COMMANDMENTS

THE TOP TEN
LEADERSHIP
COMMANDMENTS

לא תרצה   אנכי ה'
לא תנאף   לא יהיה
לא תגנב   לא תשא
לא תענה   זכור את
לא תחמד   כבד את

HANS FINZEL

David C Cook®
transforming lives together

THE TOP TEN LEADERSHIP COMMANDMENTS
Published by David C Cook
4050 Lee Vance View
Colorado Springs, CO 80918 U.S.A.

David C Cook Distribution Canada
55 Woodslee Avenue, Paris, Ontario, Canada N3L 3E5

David C Cook U.K., Kingsway Communications
Eastbourne, East Sussex BN23 6NT, England

The graphic circle C logo is a registered trademark of David C Cook.

Unless otherwise noted, all Scripture quotations are taken from the Holy Bible,
New International Version®, NIV®. Copyright © 1973, 1978, 1984 by Biblica,
Inc™. Used by permission of Zondervan. All rights reserved worldwide. www.
zondervan.com. Scripture quotations marked NLT are taken from the New Living
Translation of the Holy Bible. New Living Translation copyright © 1996, 2004
by Tyndale Charitable Trust. Used by permission of Tyndale House Publishers;
NKJV are taken from the New King James Version. Copyright © 1982 by Thomas
Nelson, Inc. Used by permission. All rights reserved; MSG are taken from THE
MESSAGE. Copyright © by Eugene H. Peterson 1993, 1994, 1995, 1996, 2000,
2001, 2002. Used by permission of NavPress Publishing Group; TNIV are taken
from the HOLY BIBLE, TODAY'S NEW INTERNATIONAL VERSION®.
Copyright © 2001, 2005 by Biblica®. Used by permission of Biblica®. All rights
reserved worldwide. The author has added italics to quotations for emphasis.

LCCN 2011944723
ISBN 978-0-7814-0488-4
eISBN 978-0-7814-0828-8

© 2012 Hans Finzel

The Team: Alex Field, Amy Kiechlin, Caitlyn York, Karen Athen.
Cover Design: Nick Lee
Cover Image: Shutterstock

Printed in the United States of America
First Edition 2012

1 2 3 4 5 6 7 8 9 10

123011

To our four grandchildren, Asher, Elias, Ireland, and Nicholas, and the many more to come. May these lessons I learned from Moses help empower you to become great leaders in your own generation.

AUTHOR'S DISCLAIMER

I write books on leadership
Not because I consider myself a great leader
But because I want to become a better leader.

> If your gift is to encourage others, be encouraging.
> If it is giving, give generously. If God has given you
> leadership ability, take the responsibility seriously.
> And if you have a gift for showing kindness to oth-
> ers, do it gladly. (Rom. 12:8 NLT)

I write books on leadership
Not from the classroom of academic theory
But from the crucible of the leadership trenches.

CONTENTS

PREFACE

I have a reverse bucket list. Not things I want to do before I die, but the top ten things I have done in my life so far of which I am proud. On my list are things like climbing a fourteener in Colorado with my son Mark; earning a doctorate; and personally meeting Mother Teresa in Calcutta, India, before she died. Definitely on the list is being an author and actually getting published (which first happened for me twenty-five years ago). Being an author was not anything I ever dreamed of doing when I was a kid. Writing is not about my ego but about reaching out and touching the lives of people I never get a chance to meet.

Some of the things on my reverse bucket list I did not actually do—just experienced—like seeing the births of my four children. Donna did all the work on that one; I just watched in amazement. And two of our four children, Andrew and Cambria, are twins, which is quite special! And our oldest son, Mark, and his wife, Danielle, also have twins—a girl named Ireland and a boy named Elias! Another very big bullet on my list: I was in Berlin twenty years ago when the Berlin Wall came down. I have a huge piece of the wall in my office to prove it. I call it "history's greatest prison break."

In 1986 I ran my first and only marathon in Vienna, Austria, which is surely on my top ten list. We lived in Vienna as a family for ten exciting years, and I thought it would be a fun accomplishment to run a marathon there. When I actually finished, I called my mom back in Alabama, and she asked me, "Did you win?" Ha! "Mom, I finished ... so yes, I won!"

The finish line in the Vienna marathon is one of the world's most dramatic and picturesque. The twenty-six-mile route took me around the ring road of downtown, over the Danube to the United Nations center, down the Prater Amusement Park area, and finally to the middle of Vienna to the finish line at Heldenplatz (which means "Heroes' Square"). This is the historical plaza in Vienna with a beautiful ancient arch that is the actual finish line. I made it to that Heldenplatz finish line in three hours and fifty minutes. My goals were to (a) finish the race and (b) finish in under four hours. I accomplished both ... and will never forget that moment I ran across the finish line, Donna and my kids and other friends on the sidelines, cheering me on.

It's not like I'm about to run through the finish line of life just yet, but I am thinking more and more these days about *finishing strong* in my leadership. And one never knows. As I write this, one of my colleagues, who is younger than I am, is dying of cancer and has just weeks to live. After thirty years in the leadership trenches, I'm thinking more and more about legacy. Will I finish well? Will I leave a legacy that other young leaders can follow? Most importantly, can

I mentor the younger generation with intentionality in the years I have left? That is the "why" of this book.

LEAD TO LEAVE

If you are just starting out as a leader, then it is your world to lead. If you're a seasoned leader like me, then take up the charge of *leading to leave*. Whatever your age, you can pour yourself into the new young leaders coming up behind you (there's a lot more on that in chapter 8). However, we boomers are approaching our sunset years of leadership, and the sun is just rising for you younger leaders. There are lessons to be learned from older leaders like Moses, lessons that can help emerging leaders lead for the long haul. I don't expect those of you in the next generation to lead the same way I've led, but I do expect you to want to finish well as you head for your own finish line.

Soon all of the organizations the older leaders currently run will be handed over to the emerging generation of leaders. We are in that very season in our ministry with my recent decision to launch a succession plan for my replacement. Whether you are an older leader running a church, a business, a local government, or a nonprofit, the great generational changing of the guard is upon us. I am excited about what I see on the horizon. Those of us currently in leadership aren't in trouble—bright new leaders are emerging everywhere. *Leading to leave* is not about clinging to a position but paving the way for future leaders.

The current generation of leaders has a torch to pass. In the time I have left as a leader in our ministry, my number one passion is to help make a way for emerging leaders. I want to serve them and offer a few grains of wisdom for the journey.

I predict one thing will hold true for these future leaders, as it has for my generation and those before us: *Many will start, but few will finish strong.*

LEADERS MAKE THINGS HAPPEN

I have enjoyed a lifetime of studying the practice of leadership and the lives of great leaders. Leaders make things happen. History is the story of leaders good and bad who have moved the world in directions both good and bad. We live in desperate times in which we need great new servant leaders to rise up and push aside self-centered leadership. Paul (one of the great leaders of the early church movement) affirms your desire to be a great leader for our times in his letter to his apprentice Timothy: "This is a trustworthy saying: 'If someone aspires to be an elder [or overseer], he desires an honorable position'" (1 Tim. 3:1 NLT).

I have the gift of leadership, and I enjoy it *most* of the time. At times it is a burden, but it is also a joy to make an impact through others. I take this leadership challenge from Paul the apostle seriously:

> If your gift is to encourage others, be encouraging.
> If it is giving, give generously. If God has given you
> leadership ability, take the responsibility seriously.
> And if you have a gift for showing kindness to

others, do it gladly.
(Rom. 12:8 NLT)

This passage says to me, "Hans—you need to work on your leadership gift. You are a leader with God-given capacity and God-given responsibility—so take charge, and keep sharpening your skills." And do it with great *diligence*. The word *diligence* means "conscientiousness in paying proper attention to a task, persevering determination to perform a task."[1] That's it!

Leadership isn't always easy. In fact, if I am honest, it's rarely

> IF YOU'VE EVER WANTED TO QUIT AS A LEADER, THIS BOOK IS FOR YOU. IF YOU ARE JUST ABOUT READY TO BOLT, THIS BOOK IS A MUST READ.... GETTING BOGGED DOWN IS A NATURAL PART OF THE LEADERSHIP JOURNEY, BUT THE KEY IS TO GET BACK UP, GET UNSTUCK, AND KEEP GOING.... MOSES HAS A LOT TO SAY TO YOU.

easy and can often be extremely discouraging. If you've ever wanted to quit as a leader, this book is for you. If you are just about ready to bolt, this book is a must read. Maybe you recently left a discouraging dead-end role, and you're trying to recover. I have met a lot of leaders like you! There is hope for your recovery, and you can eventually finish strong. Getting bogged down is a natural part of the leadership journey, but the key is to get back up, get unstuck, and keep going. You will be judged not by how many times you fall but by how well you get up. Moses has a lot to say to you. Will you join me on this journey, as we sit at the feet of this great leader, Moses?

Perhaps you're just starting out as a young leader filled with dreams of changing the world. Bravo! I have four young adult children who all seem to be at that stage in their lives. I love seeing the passion and enthusiasm of young leaders. The sad thing is how many of these leaders bail in their forties and fifties and give up on their dreams of influence.

Leaders make things happen, and people try to stop them. Not only do we fight our internal life struggles; we also bear the frustrations of others who can wear us down with unrealistic expectations. Most of the time, leaders give up on trying to win the battle of expectations and finally just quit. It seems to me that discouragement is one of the strongest tools Satan uses to try to take us out.

Have you ever wanted to leave or give up? Of course you have if you are breathing, and you are a leader. If not—trust me—it will happen before you know it. Moses wanted to quit the day he started, then again in week two, month two, and year two! Leadership can be a brutal business in any setting. Is it any wonder so many throw in the towel and go do something else? Recently, in one of the doctoral classes I teach, I had an interesting conversation with a young thirty-something pastor who leads a cutting-edge church. He disagreed with me on the above point, saying, "Hans, it will not happen to us. We have this whole church leadership thing figured out in a new way." Sounds just like the way I felt when I was thirtysomething! If you feel the same way he does, you might want to read on just in case.

Pastors of local churches are a unique breed of leader facing a host of challenges. I've always felt that being a senior pastor is the hardest job in God's service on the planet. According to recent research, there are six main reasons why pastors leave the ministry, all of which are relevant to our wider discussion of leadership:

> I felt drained by the demands on me. (58 percent of respondents listed as "great importance" or "somewhat important")
> I felt lonely or isolated. (51 percent)
> I felt bored or constrained in the position. (43 percent)
> I was not supported by denominational officials. (43 percent)
> I found a better job outside of pastoral ministry. (38 percent)
> I had marital or personal relationship problems. (27 percent)[2]

Finishing Well, Finishing Strong

I start with a simple assumption: I hope that all of us leaders want to finish well with our integrity intact. That is why I admire the long track record of Moses. If he went through all that he did and still didn't quit, what am I complaining about? He finished his "calling." I suppose the very term *calling* is very old school, but I still think it works. In my mind, calling is about following a higher purpose in life. It is listening to and obeying God's whisper. I personally define calling as "following the most compelling of many options at any cost." I have met men and women who gave up their callings, and every time this happens I see a life disappointed. I unpack this issue of calling more fully in the last chapter of this book, "Thou Shalt Keep Thine Eyes on the Prize." It takes a lifetime to build a strong leadership reputation and less than an hour to destroy it. And for many who quit, it's not the failure of their integrity that got the best of them; it was plain and simple discouragement over a long period of time. This is the place where Moses has so much to teach on enduring leadership.

During a long dark period of my leadership about a decade ago, I finally wrote my letter of resignation from my organization. I'd served as president for a long stretch of time. I was beyond the seven-year itch, and in fact it was my tenth anniversary year when I hit the bottom. Tough people problems (are there any other kind?) and personal assaults wore me out. I felt personally inadequate and at the end of my rope at the bottom of a dark cave of despair. And I wrote an amazing resignation letter too! After I spent months tweaking it, it was three pages long. In this letter addressed to my board of directors, I poured out all the frustrations and anger that I felt about being trapped in my position as CEO. I had been attacked, was burned out, and believed my job was too big for one man. No one understood what I was going through, and I felt trapped in a job that didn't maximize my gifting. I was stuck in a place that seemed very far from that ideal "sweet spot" where gifts and position merge in leadership bliss. Like Moses, I told God, "Get someone else for this impossible job!"

Fortunately, I never mailed that letter because I would have missed the good things that happened right around the corner.

Thomas Edison was a leader who refused to give up. He said, "Many of life's failures are people who did not realize how close they were to success when they gave up." And I found this to be true.

For me, it was cathartic to put my frustration in writing. I highly recommend the exercise just to get your heart down on paper. To this day, I still have the letter on my laptop, and looking back, I'm so glad that I chose not to send it. The letter has become part of my journal, not my backup plan. Harry Truman was well known for venting his frustration and anger in letters, especially during his presidency. Most of the time he never sent them, but the act of writing out his frustrations helped him process his emotions. He wrote some incredibly emotional, intense, and sometimes angry letters that can be found in David McCullough's great book *Truman*.

> MANY OF LIFE'S FAILURES ARE PEOPLE WHO DID NOT REALIZE HOW CLOSE THEY WERE TO SUCCESS WHEN THEY GAVE UP.
> —THOMAS EDISON

What made me not send my letter? Moses.

I was in the middle of a teaching assignment on leadership lessons from the life of Moses and spent months investigating his story. God met me through the story of this ancient leader, and his life encouraged me not to throw in the towel. I saw that my problems were nothing compared to his; and in reading about his perseverance, I gained the faith to go on. I am sure that he wrote many more resignation letters to God than I ever dreamed of writing to my board.

Many good things happened through my leadership in these subsequent years. I am so glad I didn't resign in that darkest hour, which came just before the dawn. Some of my greatest accomplishments in leadership came after that discouraging time. In recent months, I have chosen to finish up this leadership assignment, but the choice did not come from the dark valley of discouragement but rather the call of my heart to move to a new assignment. I unpack that decision later in this book.

The story of Moses illustrates the powerful life impact of faithful endurance. I relate to his problems, and I admire his willingness to work his way through them in partnership with God. In addition to the Ten Commandments we all know about, I have also observed ten compelling leadership "commandments" practiced by Moses.

So where can we learn how to be great leaders? To whom do we turn for the best advice on finishing strong? I don't believe we find the keys at Harvard or any other MBA program, and most management consultants really don't help all that much. Just observe the thoughts of Matthew Stewart from his book *The Management Myth*. Stewart, a career management consultant, observes, "How can so many who know so little make so much [money] by telling other people how to do the jobs they are paid to know how to do?"[3] He goes on to say, "Throughout the years I spent consulting, I never lost the sensation that I was just making it up as I went along."[4] Reading his book helped confirm a suspicion I have developed over the years—that most consultants really just tell me the time of day using my own watch!

So where do we look for the best advice on leadership? The people who can best teach us how to be great leaders are … *great leaders.*

Great leaders in history—like Abraham Lincoln, Winston Churchill, Martin Luther King Jr., Nelson Mandela, Golda Meir, Billy Graham, and Mother Teresa—endured great hardship and stayed in the fight and finished strong. If we are Christ followers, what better place to look than the Bible and a story like that of Moses, the "man of God." I've found a deep treasure of leadership insights in the story of his life, and I want to share that treasure with you now.

INTRODUCTION TO MOSES: BIG LESSONS FROM AN EPIC LIFE

Since then, no prophet has risen in Israel like Moses, whom the LORD knew face to face, who did all those miraculous signs and wonders the LORD sent him to do in Egypt—to Pharaoh and to all his officials and to his whole land. For no one has ever shown the mighty power or performed the awesome deeds that Moses did in the sight of all Israel. (Deut. 34:10–12)

If you were to draw a horizontal timeline of your leadership journey on a whiteboard, I am certain it would be a wavy line with numerous ups and downs. As rewarding as leadership is, it can be a highly frustrating occupation. We have up days and down days, great months and lousy months, and up years and down years. During those most discouraging years in my leadership journey, I immersed myself in the life of Moses. I read everything in the entire Bible written about him and by him. I was attracted to him by his troubles. Misery loves company, and he was just the man I wanted to spend time with—so I got to know him as a friend. And this friend encouraged me to stick with my leadership challenge and not give up. Eventually, I figured that if he could handle what he went through, my problems were completely insignificant!

MY OWN STORY

My life so far is not what I would classify as an epic like that of Moses' life. But it has been dramatic, with many unexpected twists and turns. In this section, I want to introduce you to Moses, but a few words about my story will set a good context. Throughout this book, I weave in and out of Moses' story to demonstrate lessons applied in my own story. I hope that my intersections with his journey will speak to your story.

When I am introduced to speak—"Hans Finzel, who lived in Austria with his family for a decade"—most audiences assume that I will have a German accent. I can fake it really well and often do! But the honest truth is that I was born and raised in Huntsville, Alabama, and the last thing in the world that I ever thought I would do is what I'm doing now. I set out to serve myself, but God changed my plans. Can you relate? A life following hard after God is filled with surprises.

I am a child of immigrants. My mom and dad had those thick German accents until the day they died. German is my "Muttersprache"—my mother tongue—which I learned even before I learned English. My father was a rocket engineer. He and over one hundred other German scientists and engineers were captured by the US Army after World War II and were brought to America to work in our space program. In 1950 they relocated to Huntsville, where I was born. NASA was created in the early 1960s, and my dad had an amazing career helping us reach the moon. It just goes to show that you don't have to be a rocket scientist to be the son of one!

I did not like being the German immigrant boy because I wanted to be normal. I hated my name. We spoke German in our home and ate strange food and had non-Alabama customs for everything. Instead of Santa Claus, we had Saint Nicholas, who came to our house to bring chocolate and fill our shoes at Christmas. Weird, huh? I rebelled as a teenager in the 1960s and got into drugs and a very destructive lifestyle that I am not proud of. You can do a lot of self-inflicted damage by the time you are eighteen. I was a full-fledged long-haired hippie who heard Led Zeppelin, Jimi Hendrix, and Janis Joplin live in concert. I knew that there was something missing in my life, but my parents did not have the answer, so I looked everywhere else.

The year 1969 changed my life forever. That year started out lousy but ended up being life changing. Just the other day I bought a *Time* magazine book entitled *1969: Woodstock, the Moon and Manson: The Turbulent End of the '60s.* Reading the book, I was reminded of what a year of contrasts it was in the formation of my generation: It was the year of the first moon landing, Woodstock, the inauguration of Richard Nixon, the assassination of Robert Kennedy, the Manson murders, and the stardom of quarterback Joe Namath. For me it was for sure the end of my personal turbulence and the year that Hans Finzel changed forever.

In the summer of 1969 my friends and I piled in my VW Bug and drove to Woodstock but never made it. We got so stoned driving up from Alabama that we made it as far as Charlotte, checked into a motel for the weekend, and had our own little Woodstock. That was as low as I ever got. I was a rebel without a cause. I knew the world was screwed up, I knew my life was a dead end, but I had no clue what to do about it. That fall, when I went off to college at the University of Alabama in Tuscaloosa, I met a group of Christ followers who told me God loved me and had a wonderful plan for my life.

In January 1970 I decided to follow Jesus and told Him that if He would take me, I would be His for life. Following Him changed everything in my life. He gave me as my life verse Isaiah 53:4–6, which basically says that He went through hell so I could have heaven. I got cleaned up (He gave me the power), went through college, and then attended seminary. I found my calling and charged after it with all that was within me. I also found my life mate, Donna. We met my senior year in college, and we decided to serve God as a team—she shared my passion to change the world. We got married and headed off to seminary together. After that, we worked in a church for a while in Southern California. But we were restless and felt we needed to write a bigger story with our lives. So we followed a dream and moved to Vienna, Austria. Our mission there was to help train church leaders behind the Iron Curtain during the dark days of communism. We were fighting for truth and God and freedom in the most oppressed place on earth at that time. Along the way, God blessed us with four wonderful children: Mark, Jeremy, Andrew, and Cambria.

Then the story changed. Who would have anticipated that the Iron Curtain would fall and the Berlin Wall would come down? As

OUR MISSION THERE WAS TO HELP TRAIN CHURCH LEADERS BEHIND THE IRON CURTAIN DURING THE DARK DAYS OF COMMUNISM.

I mentioned in the preface, I was there on November 9, 1989, to witness history's greatest prison break. Once communism fell, everything changed in Europe, and my sending organization, now called WorldVenture, asked me to come home to serve in a larger leadership role. I guess God decided to increase my horizons. I want to clarify one important thing here to which many of you might relate. I did not seek the job. We were happy in the trenches of our assignment and not interested in returning to the home office. Moses faced a similar journey when he was recruited.

After a decade in the trenches with leaders in Eastern Europe, we moved to the home office to provide leadership to leaders all over the world. I now work to help our leaders in over seventy countries become more effective. I am still amazed when I think about the little German boy from Huntsville who has had the unique honor to be in such a place of influence, entrusted with such great leadership responsibility.

In 1970 I became a "Jesus Freak" and decided that Jesus was the only way. We held up one pointing finger to symbolize our faith. What I find really uplifting is that forty years later I still believe that Jesus is the only way, and I'm still a Jesus freak. And now my greatest passion is to mentor young leaders who will take my place when I cross the finish line.

THE STORY OF MOSES

My story is tiny when held up against the story of Moses. But our stories intersect because we both serve the same God. I first learned about Moses when I was not yet a teenager. When I was a kid, I loved to go to the Saturday matinees at the movie theater. They were supercheap then, but I don't think they're a bargain anymore. I remember going with my sister, Ursula, to see every movie that Elvis ever made back when he churned out dozens of movies. He cranked out thirty-one movies from 1956 to 1969, averaging about two to three movies a year.

However, one of my favorite movies of all time was *The Ten Commandments*. *The Ten Commandments* was a 1956 motion picture that dramatized the biblical story of Moses, the adopted Egyptian prince-turned-deliverer of the Hebrew slaves. Paramount Pictures released the film on October 5, 1956. It was directed by Cecil B. DeMille and starred Charlton Heston as Moses.

What makes a great movie is the story: We like to see a character overcome great conflict to achieve a goal. Moses, the protagonist in this movie, went up first against Pharaoh and later against his own people to achieve God's purpose. His challenge was to fulfill the calling of God to rescue the Hebrew slaves out of Egypt and bring them to the Promised Land. God wanted something for His people, and He called Moses to deliver.

The story of Moses is epic, but what makes it so? The dictionary defines the word *epic* as "very imposing or impressive; a long poem or story telling of a hero's deeds."[1] Moses fit the label *hero* like a glove. In a hero's tale, the main character is often attempting to achieve the impossible at great cost and sacrifice. Moses sacrificed all the benefits that were once his as prince of Egypt for the good of the people he would lead. Would he make it? Would he overcome all the obstacles in his way?

If you surveyed people all over the planet on name recognition, Moses would be well recognized. It's amazing to me how well known he is to people of all faiths and of so many cultures of the world. Recently, *USA Today* ran a two-page spread on the popularity of Moses, which blew my mind as I read the article on an airplane. The article discussed research conducted by author Bruce Feiler on the impact of Moses on US history:

> Jesus is most certainly present and influential in people's lives in a vastly Christian nation. But when it comes to shaping the character of American self-identity, Moses is the man, Feiler says....
>
> "Moses raises questions of who is your real authority. He raises the dream of a Promised Land on Earth and escape from oppression. He's also about falling short. He never reaches that Promised Land himself. But he builds a nation ruled by law" to go forward without him....
>
> Moses fits America in every age, Feiler says.
>
> For 20 generations, his story has transcended "all our rivalries, political and religious—Democrats and Republicans, Christians and Jews and unbelievers, slaves and masters, men and women."

MOSES SACRIFICED ALL THE BENEFITS THAT WERE ONCE HIS ... FOR THE GOOD OF THE PEOPLE HE WOULD LEAD.

Even now, as the Bible is less commonly read,
Moses still thrives, detached from his scriptural
moorings.[2]

THREE ACTS IN THE EPIC STORY

The story of the leadership of Moses in these forty years of drama is
a true epic. If it were a play, it would consist of three acts, with each
act making up a neat span of forty years.

ACT ONE: MAN OF POWER (BIRTH TO AGE FORTY)

Moses was born of Jewish parents during a time of purging; he
was saved by his mom and raised as a son of Pharaoh in preparation
for his future leadership.

Acts 7:20–22 says this: "At that time Moses was born, and he
was no ordinary child. For three months he was cared for in his
father's house. When he was placed outside, Pharaoh's daughter
took him and brought him up as her own son. Moses was educated
in all the wisdom of the Egyptians and was powerful in speech and
action."

ACT TWO: MAN OF WEAKNESS (AGES FORTY TO EIGHTY)

Before he was fit to be of service to God, he had to get his
"BD Degree." This is what I call the "back of the desert" degree.
Moses was still too full of himself and needed to be broken so
that he could develop the humility he would need to be a servant

leader. It reminds me of Romans 12:3: "For by the grace given to me I say to every one of you: Do not think of yourself more highly than you ought, but rather think of yourself with sober judgment, in accordance with the measure of faith God has given you." Paul wrote those words because he'd been in the desert, and he, too, had been a man with a huge ego.

Moses thought he was ready for his shining moment of great deliverance when he was forty years old. But he failed miserably and lacked God's power. He lacked a lot of things that would be developed in his years in the wilderness. I have seen this same tendency in a lot of young leaders.

Acts 7:23–29 says:

> BEFORE HE WAS FIT TO BE OF SERVICE TO GOD, HE HAD TO GET HIS "BD DEGREE." THIS IS WHAT I CALL THE "BACK OF THE DESERT" DEGREE. MOSES WAS STILL TOO FULL OF HIMSELF AND NEEDED TO BE BROKEN SO THAT HE COULD DEVELOP THE HUMILITY HE WOULD NEED TO BE A SERVANT LEADER.

When Moses was forty years old, he decided to visit his fellow Israelites. He saw one of them being mistreated by an Egyptian, so he went to his defense and avenged him by killing the Egyptian. Moses thought that his own people would realize that God was using him to rescue them, but they did not. The next day Moses came upon two Israelites who were fighting. He tried to reconcile them by saying, "Men, you are brothers; why do you want to hurt each other?"

But the man who was mistreating the other pushed Moses aside and said, "Who made you ruler and judge over us? Do you want to kill me as you killed the Egyptian yesterday?" When Moses heard this, he fled to Midian, where he settled as a foreigner and had two sons.

ACT THREE: MAN OF GOD (AGES EIGHTY TO ONE HUNDRED TWENTY)

It was not until he was eighty that Moses was truly ready to lead. Thankfully, that is an outdated paradigm! I would have hated to wait until the end of my life to start leading. But there are so many lessons on preparation to draw out of these years of Moses' life, as God removes hindrances from him and builds into him the traits he will need.

Acts 7:30–38 says:

After forty years had passed, an angel appeared to Moses in the flames of a burning bush in the desert near Mount Sinai. When he saw this, he was amazed at the sight. As he went over to look more closely, he heard the Lord's voice: "I am the God of your fathers, the God of Abraham, Isaac and Jacob." Moses trembled with fear and did not dare to look.

Then the Lord said to him, "Take off your sandals; the place where you are standing is holy ground. I have indeed seen the oppression of my people in Egypt. I have heard their groaning and have come down to set them free. Now come, I will send you back to Egypt."

This is the same Moses whom they had rejected with the words, "Who made you ruler and judge?" He was sent to be their ruler and deliverer by God himself, through the angel who appeared to him in the bush. He led them out of Egypt and did wonders and miraculous signs in Egypt, at the Red Sea and for forty years in the desert.

This is that Moses who told the Israelites, "God will send you a prophet like me from your own people." He was in the assembly in the desert, with the angel who spoke to him on Mount Sinai, and with our fathers; and he received living words to pass on to us.

I can't think of anyone in biblical history—or the entire history of the human race, for that matter—who had a more difficult leadership challenge than Moses. Of the sixty-six books of the Bible, Moses is mentioned in thirty-two of them! Moses is mentioned in twenty books of the Old Testament and twelve books of the New Testament. He was a man of great importance to God's plan and to God's people. Let's review a few basic facts of this extraordinary life.

WHAT MAKES MOSES SO EPIC?

The backstory begins with Joseph, over four hundred years earlier. It was Joseph who brought the Hebrews into Egypt in the first place. Genesis 46:2–4 says:

> And God spoke to Israel in a vision at night and said, "Jacob! Jacob!"
> "Here I am," he replied.
> "I am God, the God of your father," he said. "Do not be afraid to go down to Egypt, for I will make you into a great nation there. I will go down to Egypt with you, and I will surely bring you back again. And Joseph's own hand will close your eyes."

Joseph was used by God to get the family of Jacob and his twelve sons to Egypt because the time was not right for them to settle in the Promised Land. Moses was the instrument that fulfilled the promise God made to Jacob in Genesis 46. God's promise to Jacob that "I will surely bring you back again" would be fulfilled through Moses. In Exodus 3:9–10 God cast the job description for Moses for the next forty years, though Moses did not know it at the time: "And now the cry of the Israelites has reached me, and I have seen the way the Egyptians are oppressing them. So now, go. I am sending you to Pharaoh to bring my people the Israelites out of Egypt."

During their 430 years in Egypt, the Hebrews grew from a dozen sons to over two million people! In the time between Joseph getting them into Egypt and Moses taking them out, they had grown from a family to the size of a small country. And you think you have too many things to manage?

For forty years Moses led a group of people that he did not want to lead in a task for which he never volunteered. From day one, Moses' own people resisted his leadership. He faced betrayal from friends and enemies alike. Moses wanted to quit on recruitment day and certainly long before the Hebrews ever left Egypt. But for reasons that become obvious in the story, Moses was the right selection. I think that, early on, Moses had a keen understanding of the leadership challenge that lay ahead.

After an amazing start, Moses actually demonstrated forty years of effective leadership. Moses pulled off the impossible. He led the children of Israel out of Egypt, across the Red Sea, through the wilderness of Sinai, and to the doorstep of the Promised Land. He had his failures along the way, but he got his people there. And how he got them there is the story. Their trip to the Promised Land probably should have taken a year on foot—and if we were to drive the distance today on a freeway, we could do it in one day! But it took forty years because the people and their leader weren't ready.

In Moses' leadership journey, God worked on Moses' character to make him one of the greatest leaders in biblical history. And the journey was the reward! I love D. L. Moody's summary of Moses' life:

> Moses spent his first forty years thinking he was somebody. He spent his second forty years learning he was a nobody. He spent his third forty years discovering what God can do with a nobody.[3]

THE TEN LEADERSHIP COMMANDMENTS

Today, publishers seem to approach every leader who is on the public stage to write a book. If Moses were alive today, surely he'd have more than one best seller. If he had been asked to write a book on leadership, the principles in this book might be his top ten leadership lessons. Moses practiced leadership for the long haul. In addition to the Ten Commandments he received from God on tablets, I've observed ten compelling leadership commandments he practiced throughout his journey. These are not sterile classroom principles; rather they are intimate real-life coaching tips that I have tried to practice in my own leadership journey. Sometimes we are asked to lead in situations that we don't fully understand, in an arena that perhaps doesn't appeal to us humanly, for outcomes only fully understood by God.

> SOMETIMES WE ARE ASKED TO LEAD IN SITUATIONS THAT WE DON'T FULLY UNDERSTAND, IN AN ARENA THAT PERHAPS DOESN'T EVEN APPEAL TO US HUMANLY, FOR OUTCOMES ONLY FULLY UNDERSTOOD BY GOD.

Ever since I wrote the book *The Top Ten Mistakes Leaders Make*, I've been a huge fan of top ten lists. When I wrapped up my study of the life of Moses, I reflected on all I had learned and came up with my top ten reasons why I love this man. Throughout this book, we will see time and again how these observations come through in his leadership journey.

Top Ten Things I Love About Moses

1. His leadership was characterized by faith and obedience: Trust and obey—it's the only way.

2. He was not seeking to lead, but he was *willing* to lead.

3. He succeeded as a reluctant leader.

4. He led with strength bathed in humility—a true servant leader.

5. He was not perfect! He overcame his weaknesses.

6. He never gave up through the darkest hours of discouragement.

7. He overcame his fickle, reluctant followers.

8. He grew as a person—he listened to feedback and displayed strong personal development.

9. He was a man of the Word of God!

10. He was a man of prayer—he listened to God, and he is one of the few people who actually have seen the face of God.

Okay, so I hope I've convinced you if you weren't convinced before. Moses is a big deal. He was back when he rescued God's people, and he is today. He lived an epic life that can teach us about leadership and finishing strong. And yes, I will get to the topic of his failure, which kept him from setting foot into the Promised Land. I have to save some drama for later! Now let's dig into the story.

Bible References on the Life of Moses

Where to Read His Story in the Bible
Old Testament

Exodus 2—20: Moses in Egypt

Exodus 24: Moses speaking to God on Mount Sinai

Exodus 31:18—34: Moses receiving the Ten Commandments; idolatry in the camp; and the second tablets

Exodus 35—40: Building of the ark, other holy implements, and the tabernacle

Leviticus: Giving of the laws and ordinances

Numbers 9:15—10: The cloud and pillar of fire; departure from Sinai

Numbers 11: The people complaining about manna; quail; judgment

Numbers 12: Dissension of Aaron and Miriam

Numbers 13: Spies sent into Canaan

Numbers 14: Israelites refusing to enter the land

Numbers 16: Rebellion of Korah

Numbers 17: Budding of Aaron's rod

Numbers 20: Moses' disobedience in striking the rock

Numbers 21:4–9: People judged; bronze serpent

Numbers 25: People's immorality at Moab; judgment

Numbers 27:12–23: Moses preparing to die, seeing the land; Joshua chosen to succeed

Numbers 31: Vengeance on Midianites

Numbers 32: Some tribes settling conquered lands east of Jordan

Numbers 33:50–56: Moses giving instructions for the conquest of Canaan

Deuteronomy 1—11: Moses rehearsing history of deliverance, giving commands

Deuteronomy 27—30: Moses pronouncing blessings and curses on Israel

Deuteronomy 31: Anointing of Joshua to lead Israel

Deuteronomy 32: Moses' imminent death; song of Moses

Deuteronomy 33: Moses giving final blessings on Israel

Deuteronomy 34: Death of Moses, the "servant of the Lord," on Mount Nebo

Nehemiah 9:9–25: Returned Babylonian captives fasting, praying, confessing, and rehearsing history of the exodus/Moses

Psalm 90: Prayer of Moses

Psalm 105: History of God's faithfulness to Israel, deliverance from Egypt under Moses

Psalm 106: History of Israel's unfaithfulness and God's mercy from the exodus onward

New Testament

Mark 12:26–27: Jesus speaking of Moses and the burning bush

Acts 7:17–45: Stephen talking about Moses through Joshua

Hebrews 3: Jesus compared to Moses (greater than)

Hebrews 11:23–29: The faith of Moses

1

LEADERSHIP COMMANDMENT #1: THOU SHALT CLING TO THE VISION

This is the same Moses whom they had rejected with the words, "Who made you ruler and judge?" He was sent to be their ruler and deliverer by God himself, through the angel who appeared to him in the bush. He led them out of Egypt and did wonders and miraculous signs in Egypt, at the Red Sea and for forty years in the desert. (Acts 7:35–36)

Big Idea: Where there is no vision, the people don't follow.
It is as simple as that. Vision for a better future, conveyed
with genuine passion, is the great motivator.

Lack of vision can kill any organization, no matter how great it used to be. And if it's already dead, you will never bring it back to life without a megadose of fresh vision.

I had a frustrating lunch recently with a senior pastor who was nine years into his leadership journey at his church. I enjoy encouraging pastors, but this meeting was a vivid illustration of the vision problem. He's an older man in his fourth church, but sadly, the church has been on a death spiral for decades—and it's been a long, slow, and painful demise. At one time the church was over a thousand strong, but now it's down to one hundred adults, and there's hardly a young person in sight. This pastor wasn't the cause of the decline—it started long before he arrived on the scene—but he seems to be doing little to stop it. I probed and listened and tried to be of help. What I really wanted to do was stand on top of that lunch table and jump up and down, scream-ing, "They need vision! There is nothing out there in the future that is compelling people to get excited. Vision is a magnet—it draws people to our cause. People follow vision that is communi-cated with passion!" The body is lying on the gurney in the ER, gasping for its last breath, and the diagnosis is clear: "Terminal because of lack of vision."

People have to want to be helped. In the case of this pastor's church, the congregants suffer from organizational arrogance: They act like the problem is the fault of all the people who aren't coming to their church. The excuse often sounds like this: "We haven't changed in forty years; society has gone down the tubes. We are staying faith-ful to our calling." The sad thing about that lunch meeting is that the pastor has a complete lack of understanding about why the church is failing. It is a *visionless* place. Young people and young married couples stay away in droves. He told me about a small tweak that he is making in the programs, but his description showed he was in "maintenance mode"—totally visionless and clinging to something that no longer exists.

As we finished our long lunch, I could tell that he didn't really want honest feedback on the problem. I concluded that he is coasting to retirement, he does not want to rock the boat at this stage in his career, and he lays the blame at the feet of the people, not at his own lack of leadership.

> A LEADER IS ONE WHO SEES MORE THAN OTHERS SEE, WHO SEES FARTHER THAN OTHERS SEE, AND WHO SEES BEFORE OTHERS DO.
> —LeRoy Eims, *Be the Leader You Were Meant to Be*

Where there is no vision, the people won't follow. Vision for a better future is the great motivator. Job number one for leaders is to cast vision. In the book *The Leadership Challenge*, the authors write, "Leaders are pioneers. They are people who venture into unexplored territory. They guide us to new and often unfamiliar destinations. People who take the lead are the foot soldiers in the campaigns for change. The unique reason for having leaders—their differentiating function—is to move us forward. Leaders get us going someplace."[1]

Moses was given a vision from God that first day at the burning bush. It was a vision of the Promised Land. In Exodus 3:7–8 we read: "The LORD said, 'I have indeed seen the misery of my people in Egypt. I have heard them crying out because of their slave drivers, and I am concerned about their suffering. So I have come down to rescue them from the hand of the Egyptians and to bring them up out of that land into a good and spacious land, a land flowing with milk and honey—the home of the Canaanites, Hittites, Amorites, Perizzites, Hivites and Jebusites.'"

Another way to look at vision is what I call the "passion factor." People follow passion, *not facts*. If you set yourself on fire, people will come to watch you burn. People follow leaders who know where they are going and who convince others to go with them. Ronald Reagan was known as that kind of a leader. As president he was called "the great communicator." And what did he communicate? Reagan communicated a fresh *vision* for America that would end the Cold War. Steve Jobs was a technological visionary who changed the world several times over through his products. Nelson Mandela is a political visionary who changed the face of South Africa. Vision for the future is the goal—the prize—the motivation that the leader keeps in front of the people. For Moses, the vision was to reach the Promised Land, and barriers kept the Hebrews from that goal for forty years! People follow leaders who are going somewhere they wish to go!

> A LEADER IS ANYONE WHO HAS TWO CHARACTERISTICS: FIRST HE IS GOING SOMEPLACE: SECOND, HE IS ABLE TO PERSUADE OTHER PEOPLE TO GO WITH HIM.
> —W. H. COWLEY, STANFORD UNIVERSITY

Catharine is an amazing visionary leader in our ministry in Uganda, East Africa. She leads a ministry called Hope Alive!, which serves "child-headed households." Frankly, up until the time I visited

Uganda, I was not aware how many families in Africa are parent-
less. Often, the oldest sibling serves as the parent because the actual
parents died of AIDS, disappeared in the war, or just abandoned
the children because of extreme poverty. In many cases there never
were parents—just a mother who kept having children for whom
she could not care. These are the fragile little family units we call
"child-headed households." The family might consist of a twelve-
year-old brother or sister taking care of his or her siblings and trying
to find food and shelter. Catharine became aware of the problem
after visiting many villages and finding these little households. What
she witnessed firsthand broke her heart. One of the biggest problems
is that the children cannot go to school because they do not have
shoes or school supplies or the minimal amount of money required
for school registration. They have no money. So Catharine began
to raise money, supply those things to give some structure to these
fragile families, and provide some basic food, necessities, and the
registration fees for school.

You might think that it was easy to start helping these kids—
that they would welcome Catharine's help with open arms. That was
not always the case. In the past, people had betrayed these children,
making promises and later vanishing like the morning dew on a hot
summer day.

Catharine made a trip up to northern Uganda and gathered
hundreds of children under a grove of trees to talk to them about
a vision for going to school. Unlike some American kids who may
not like school (like me when I was a kid!), these kids would give
anything to go to school. There is nothing else to do in their villages.
And without school, they are destined for poverty and are left behind

in every way. Catharine told them her vision of what she wanted to provide for them. To her surprise, when she finished, there was no response and no enthusiasm—the children just sat there with blank stares on their faces. At that point one of the older boys stood up to tell her, "These children have heard too many promises. They have no hope that anything will change. You will not come back to our village. What you say is what we need, but we have no hope that anything will change."

Catharine proved them wrong. She did come back! Month after month, she and her team came. They now supply the children with shoes, textbooks, shelter, and school registration every year.

The transformation in the countenances of the children was striking when Catharine came back as she promised. In their faces and on their tongues was *hope!* Years have passed in which Catharine has faithfully fulfilled that vision. The children even wrote a song to Catharine to thank her for the vision that she brought to their lives. Here are the lyrics to "We Are Children of Hope":

> We are happy, very happy to receive you our dear visitors;
> *We welcome you to our project of hope, Hope Alive!*
> Aunt Catharine, you are here.
> *Keep, keep on coming and promote our project of hope,*
> *Hope Alive!*
> We are the Children of Hope,
> O God, hear our burden;
> We cry out to You,
> *We are the Children of Hope.*

Catharine created a vision for the ministry. If you are the founder of the group you lead, then you pursue your vision. But most of us inherit vision or create new vision from the ground up. The pastor I referred to at the beginning of this chapter is in a typical situation. He, like most pastors, did not plant a church but inherited a congregation. In some cases pastors go to churches that already have a compelling vision in place. The search committee looks for a leader to help it fulfill the church's existing vision. But I've observed that this is not usually the case. Most new leaders taking on a new assignment have to get to know the situation and then begin to cast a new vision for the future. I find that search committees, by and large, look for leaders with fresh vision. Most of us have to begin by asking God to help us create new vision from scratch.

VISION HAS TO ENDURE OVER TIME

When do people need vision? When did Moses have to cast vision? How about at the beginning, the middle, *and* the end! We don't know a lot about what Moses did during his forty years in the wilderness between the ages of forty and eighty, but I am convinced that he got the vision. By the time he went back to Egypt to deliver the Israelites, he was clear about the future, and no matter what happened, nobody was able to wrestle that vision out of his heart. His example has been a constant reminder to me that I have to do the same thing with my people. Yes, there are many other important principles that I cover in other chapters of this book, but I believe the number one desperate need is for people to hear a compelling vision from their leaders.

MISSION AND VISION STATEMENTS ARE ...
- *LIKE GLUE*—THEY HELP LEADERS HOLD AN ORGANIZATION TOGETHER.
- *LIKE A MAGNET*—THEY ATTRACT NEWCOMERS AS MEMBERS, EMPLOYEES, CUSTOMERS, OR DONORS.
- *LIKE A YARDSTICK*—THEY ALLOW A LEADER TO MEASURE HOW HIS OR HER GROUP IS DOING.
- *LIKE A LASER*—THEY POINT YOU TO YOUR DESTINATION.

MOSES CAST VISION IN THE BEGINNING

Moses asked the Israelites to leave their homes in Egypt and to go out to a new land "flowing with milk and honey." He promised an abundant land where they would no longer be slaves. Can you imagine how amazing that must have sounded to them? It sounds like the days of the Oregon Trail, when the promise of land, peace, and freedom drew thousands to migrate west across the new frontier of America. Moses got the people to move out by sharing God's vision for a better future. He was so good at delivering the vision that they left everything in Egypt to follow his lead.

Exodus 6:6–8 says this:

> Therefore, say to the Israelites: "I am the LORD, and I will bring you out from under the yoke of the Egyptians. I will free you from being slaves to them, and I will redeem you with an outstretched arm and with mighty acts of judgment. I will take you as my

own people, and I will be your God. Then you will
know that I am the LORD your God, who brought
you out from under the yoke of the Egyptians. And
I will bring you to the land I swore with uplifted
hand to give to Abraham, to Isaac and to Jacob. I
will give it to you as a possession. I am the LORD."

MOSES KEPT THE DREAM ALIVE FOR FORTY YEARS

Throughout his leadership in the desert of Sinai, Moses painted
the vision of the Promised Land. Yes, the Israelites followed him out
of Egypt, but as is usually the case during the test of time, they lost
faith. The journey was more difficult than they expected, and it took
longer than they'd imagined. Most change initiatives I've been a part
of exhibited both of those characteristics. The toughest time is in the
muddle of the middle. The people forgot the deliverances of God
and the promises of God, and they grumbled.

Like Moses, I have found it most
difficult to keep the vision alive in the
middle years of my leadership. To start
off fresh and new is easy. It's so inspir-
ing in the front end of a new leadership
assignment to generate vision. That's
exactly what people expect of the new
leader. I was so full of vision in my first
year at my current role that we held
vision banquets all over the country to

> I HAVE FOUND IT
> MOST DIFFICULT TO
> KEEP THE VISION
> ALIVE IN THE
> MIDDLE YEARS OF
> MY LEADERSHIP.

roll out my plans. Those were exciting days. But what happens after the seven-year itch? I am now approaching two decades in leadership in my ministry, and it is at this point that I find it the toughest to keep the vision alive. Again I admire Moses for staying close to God and keeping the vision alive for forty years. With great patience he continued to remind the Israelites of where they were going: "I will establish your borders from the Red Sea to the Sea of the Philistines, and from the desert to the River. I will hand over to you the people who live in the land and you will drive them out before you" (Ex. 23:31).

MOSES MADE SURE THE VISION WOULD NOT DIE

Moses poured the vision into his protégé, Joshua, at the end of his career—when we fast-forward to the end of Moses' career, we see him transfer the vision to Joshua.

> THEN MOSES SUMMONED JOSHUA AND SAID TO HIM IN THE PRESENCE OF ALL ISRAEL, "GO AND TAKE THE LAND AND DO IT YOUR WAY!" (AUTHOR'S PARAPHRASE).

Moses knew that he would not set foot in the Promised Land, and it became clear to him that Joshua would succeed him. He knew how uncourageous most of his followers were, and he also knew that leaders make things happen, so the younger leader Joshua would have to run with the vision. Clearly, Moses imparted the dream and vision to Joshua. Here we witness the transference of vision from the older leader to the younger one. Moses accepted Joshua, endorsed his leadership openly, and believed in him.

We read about this in Deuteronomy:

Then Moses summoned Joshua and said to him in the presence of all Israel, "Be strong and courageous, for you must go with this people into the land that the LORD swore to their forefathers to give them, and you must divide it among them as their inheritance. The LORD himself goes before you and will be with you; he will never leave you nor forsake you. Do not be afraid; do not be discouraged." (Deut. 31:7–8)

MOSES REPEATED THE VISION IN THE FINAL DAYS OF HIS MINISTRY

I recommend that you read the entire chapter of Deuteronomy 33. It describes one of the great moments in the life of Moses. This chapter contains what is known as "the blessing of Moses," a passage that records Moses pronouncing his blessings on the twelve tribes of Israel before his death. He recited both the past history of the Israelites and their bright future. He also summarized the attributes of each of the twelve tribes and their leaders. How is this for passing on a grand vision?

The eternal God is your refuge,
    and underneath are the everlasting arms.
He will drive out your enemy before you,
    saying, "Destroy him!"
So Israel will live in safety alone;
    Jacob's spring is secure
in a land of grain and new wine,
    where the heavens drop dew.

Blessed are you, O Israel!
  Who is like you,
  a people saved by the LORD?
He is your shield and helper
  and your glorious sword.
Your enemies will cower before you,
  and you will trample down their high places. (Deut.
  33:27–29)

Sometimes I struggle to keep vision at the forefront of my own leadership. There are so many other demands and things that tend to distract me. I recently gave my annual state of the ministry address for a big gathering of our stakeholders. I know that a lot of pastors, CEOs, and other leaders give a similar talk at the beginning of each calendar year. I've been doing this address year after year, and I also know that people want to see what I have to say about the future. I know that they want to be excited about a positive future. Who would want to listen to a leader who shares nothing but gloom and doom?

> "IN THE ABSENCE OF GREAT DREAMS, PETTINESS PREVAILS."... A VISION WITHOUT PASSION IS JUST ANOTHER BORING IDEA.

I am usually on fire about the future. Most of my people know that I am a visionary, but this past year my message fell flat. Honestly, the weight of people problems and organizational hassles blew out the fire of my vision. So many distractions pull us leaders down. Instead of soaring with eagles, we clean up after messy pigeons. And

I know that part of the reason was my own ambivalence about our future. I have led us through so much change, and I've found that the future is a moving target. So I have to paint a different future because the world is changing. Unlike Moses, who had a concrete piece of geography as the end goal, often our goal is much more uncertain. In the world we navigate today, I feel like the finish line keeps moving!

So as I prepared my state of the ministry address, I focused on the challenges we faced. In the weeks after my talk, I had a number of our leaders ask me, "Hans, where's the vision?" I realized my mistake and began to have meetings with my top leadership team to recast some fresh vision. I learned the lesson again that my people expect me to share vision about where we are going. I cannot get bogged down and focus only on our problems. That outlook breeds negativity. A leader must cast a vision of new opportunities. People hunger for vision. It seems like they need it more than anything else we can provide as their leader. I don't know where I first heard this, but I have seen it for real: "In the absence of great dreams, pettiness prevails."

On a recent visit to my publisher in Colorado Springs, I was struck by the centerpiece of his office decorations, a large frame plaque on the wall. The caption read, "Attempt something so big, that unless God intervenes, it is bound to fail."

A CONSTANT NEED FOR FRESH VISION

Visioneering is tough work. Even—especially—if your organization is fifty or one hundred years old or older, new times require fresh expressions of the vision. WorldVenture began in 1943, and though we've had many times of rebirthing a fresh vision, we are now in the process once again. It is one of the most important disciplines of our leadership team. Even as I'm writing this, my own leadership team is exploring our future together. Things are changing so dramatically around us, and we face new opportunities and threats that weren't conceivable just five years ago.

So we find ourselves again hammering away at a fresh focus on the future. We are not changing our core values or foundational purpose for existing, but visions for the next chunk of years have to be cast fresh. It is during this time of future casting that I have come to recognize the critical need for young Joshuas and Calebs to take over the carrying of vision as I move aside. It is not fair for an older leader to hang on if the vision has grown tired. Not only unfair, but downright danger-ous! I plan to lead hard and lead strong through the finish line, but I also recognize the critical need for leadership transition. And as we are looking for our new leader, top on my list of critical performance requirements for the new person is the *ability to cast vision*. We need a leader who can cast and carry vision strongly into the future.

There is no one formula for a perfect vision statement. I like what Stephen Covey says about vision in his book *The 7 Habits of Highly Effective People*: "We are more in need of a vision or destina-tion and a compass (a set of principles or directions) and less in need of a road map."[2] Covey clarifies the difference in management and leadership when he says, "Management is efficiency in climbing the ladder of success; leadership determines whether the ladder is leaning against the right wall."[3] This takes me back to that pastor I told you about at the beginning of this chapter. He is effectively managing a local congregation that is leaning against the wrong wall, a wall of a bygone era. My job as a leader in my organization is to find the right vision and to cast it passionately.

In one of my favorite older books in my leadership library, *Visionary Leadership*, Burt Nanus defines vision as simply "a realistic, credible, attractive future for your organization.... Selecting and articulating the right vision, this powerful idea, is the toughest task and the truest test of great leadership."[4] He goes on to state that powerful and transforming visions always tend to have the following special properties:

- They are appropriate for the organization and for the times....
- They set standards of excellence and reflect high ideals....
- They clarify purpose and direction....
- They inspire enthusiasm and encourage commitment....
- They are well articulated and easily understood....
- They reflect the uniqueness of the organization....
- They are ambitious.[5]

ENEMIES OF VISION

I am so impressed that Moses kept the dream alive because he faced such dark, discouraging days, which I will unpack in later chapters. We have to honor him for keeping the vision alive amid hearts that forgot they followed the awesome God of the universe. In Psalm 106 the writer recounted just how much the people fought the vision of Moses:

When our ancestors were in Egypt,
  they gave no thought to your miracles;
they did not remember your many kindnesses,
  and they rebelled by the sea, the Red Sea.
Yet he saved them for his name's sake,
  to make his mighty power known.
He rebuked the Red Sea, and it dried up;
  he led them through the depths as through a desert.
He saved them from the hand of the foe;
  from the hand of the enemy he redeemed them.
The waters covered their adversaries;
  not one of them survived.
Then they believed his promises
  and sang his praise.

But they soon forgot what he had done
  and did not wait for his plan to unfold.
    (Ps. 106:7–13 TNIV)

The enemies of vision are real, and they are constant. I think I've experienced them all. Here are the enemies of vision that Moses faced during his forty years:

He was implementing an outlandish plan.
He did not have a lot in common with the people
he led.
He was eighty years old—not exactly a young leader.
He was unknown—did not rise up through the ranks.

There was a cultural gap between him and his followers.

He was moving people out of their comfort zone.

He had fickle followers.

Some of the strong personalities within the camp resisted his leadership.

The above list features the challenges that Moses faced, challenges that fought against his vision. As we read in Numbers 11:10, "Moses heard the people of every family wailing, each at the entrance to his tent." How could he lead in the face of all that complaining? Here is the list that I made about my own struggles to keep vision in front of my people. These are the enemies of vision I face every day:

Monday morning

The routine pressures of my job

Expectations of what others want me to do

Personal inadequacies as a leader

A changing future

Doubt about direction

Failure with past initiatives

Exhaustion and fatigue in the rank and file

Differing views of the future

Differing views of our problems

Lack of respect for leadership

Boredom with leadership—could we get a fresh face?

Politics

Pettiness

I respect long-term leaders who keep their vision alive. The biggest reason I respect Bill Hybels at Willow Creek is for his fresh vision casting within such longevity. He has been faithfully leading Willow Creek Community Church since he founded it over thirty-five years ago. It is a church that has vision. It's not a perfect church, but here's a man who knows how to cast vision. He says in his book *Axiom*, "At the core of leadership sits the power of vision, in my estimation the most potent offensive weapon in the leader's arsenal. It has been defined dozens of ways, but for me, the crispest articulation of vision is that it's a 'picture of the future that produces passion in people.'"[6] Notice how Hybels connects vision and passion—these grand visions will ignite passion in the hearts of people. A vision without passion is just another boring idea.

I've been a collector of good books on vision for decades. So I'll finish this first chapter with a selection of quotes from my collection of insights on this profound topic of vision.

> Vision for ministry is a clear mental image of a preferable future imparted by God to His chosen servants and is based upon an accurate understanding of God, self, and circumstances.
> —George Barna, *The Power of Vision*

> There is no more powerful engine driving an organization toward excellence and long-range success than an attractive, worthwhile, achievable vision for the future, widely shared.
> —Burt Nanus, *Visionary Leadership*

Twenty-first-century leaders will lead not by the
authority of their position but by their ability to
articulate a vision and core values for their organizations or congregations.
> —Aubrey Malphurs, *Values-Driven Leadership*

Vision is a clear mental picture of what could be,
fueled by the conviction that it should be.
> —Andy Stanley, *Visioneering*

If your group lacks a compelling current vision, work on getting
it. It is job number one. When the vision is clear, people begin to
move. If they are busy rowing to an exciting destination, they don't
rock the boat.

All men dream: but not equally. Those who dream
by night in the dusty recesses of their minds awake
to find that it was vanity: but the dreamers of day
are dangerous men, for they may act their dreams
with open eyes, to make it possible.
> —T. E. Lawrence, *Seven Pillars of Wisdom*

2

LEADERSHIP COMMANDMENT #2: THOU SHALT NOT SERVE THINE OWN EGO

But Moses said to God, "Who am I, that I should go to
Pharaoh and bring the Israelites out of Egypt?" (Ex. 3:11)

Now Moses was a very humble man, more humble than
anyone else on the face of the earth. (Num. 12:3)

Big Idea: Reluctance is a common trait of great leadership. It
is the foundation for humble lifelong leadership. If you find
yourself a reluctant leader, you are in good company.

"Lord, send someone else." I love this prayer because I prayed it
recently. I felt depressed all weekend and acted grouchy toward
Donna.

"Why are you so on edge?" she asked me. Then I figured it out—I was anxious about the coming week. I was going to have to be "on" all week for a packed schedule and nonstop responsibilities at our annual staff conference, with no downtime. I would deliver my annual state of the ministry talk that I mentioned in the first chapter. In addition, I would be in board meetings all week and would be spending the rest of the week with two hundred staff. I am their leader, and they all expect me to know their names and care and stop and engage them in conversation. I do love them as a leader and their shepherd, but bottom line—*I am an introvert.* I meet a lot of other leaders just like me. Why do we introverts sign up for this stuff? So this was my prayer that particular weekend: "Lord, send someone else." It is the prayer of a reluctant leader. In Exodus 4:13, Moses said, "O Lord, please send someone else to do it."

> THE PRAYER OF A RELUCTANT LEADER: "BUT MOSES SAID, 'O LORD, PLEASE SEND SOMEONE ELSE TO DO IT'" (EX. 4:13).

How many times I have prayed this prayer when I am about to do one of the following:

Deliver a challenging speaking assignment

Go into a long, tough staff meeting

Fire someone

Correct someone who reports to me

Lean in to conflict resolution

Embark on a big business trip (I travel internationally a lot)

Go into a board meeting

Lead a big, important meeting with a lot at stake

Learn that they are disappointed in my leadership

Get the results of my 360-degree evaluation by my peers

Let's pick up the story of Moses when he met God for the first time at the burning bush. It is clear in Exodus 3 that God wanted to use Moses to deliver the Israelites from their misery in Egypt. The vision was crystal clear. Just look at all of these statements that show what God wanted to do:

> The LORD said, "I have indeed seen the misery of my people in Egypt. I have heard them crying out because of their slave drivers, and I am concerned about their suffering. So I have come down to rescue them from the hand of the Egyptians and to bring them up out of that land into a good and spacious land, a land flowing with milk and honey—the home of the Canaanites, Hittites, Amorites, Perizzites, Hivites and Jebusites. And now the cry of the Israelites has reached me, and I have seen the way the Egyptians are oppressing them. So now, go. I am sending you to Pharaoh to bring [lead] my people the Israelites out of Egypt." (Ex. 3:7–10)

Here is a summary of God's main points to Moses from the burning bush:

God observes:

I have seen the misery of my people.

I have heard them crying out.

I am concerned about their suffering.

I have come down to rescue them.

The cry of the Israelites has reached me.

I have seen the way the Egyptians oppress them.

Then God assigns:

Now, go.

I am sending you to Pharaoh.

To lead my people the Israelites out of Egypt.

THE BLOWBACK BEGINS AT ONCE

There was complete clarity in God's message at the burning bush. It could not be misunderstood. But as soon as the message was delivered, Moses began to push back. We read in Exodus 3:11, "But Moses said to God, 'Who am I, that I should go to Pharaoh and bring the Israelites out of Egypt?'"

Moses was a reluctant leader from the start, and he never wanted the job God gave him. I think this is strength, not weakness. Reluctance has always been a good foundation for effective leadership. God asked Moses to lead, but Moses didn't accept the assignment until after a long dialogue and negotiations. We know in hindsight that he served faithfully out of obedience to God and a sense of duty. Moses remained true to his call despite his reluctance.

MOSES' FIVE EXCUSES TO GOD — "YOU TALKING TO ME?"

Let's look at the five excuses of Moses one by one. Moses obviously had great struggles with feeling inadequate. Can you relate?

EXCUSE #1 — THE EXCUSE OF IDENTITY

In his first excuse in Exodus 3:11, Moses told God that He had the wrong man, that He had made a mistake and appeared to the wrong person at the burning bush. Moses asked God, "Who am I?" This is like the person who looks behind himself and asks, "Who me? You talking to me? You can't be talking to me!" I think that many leaders struggle with the identity issue. Just last week, I talked with one of my leaders who struggles with his position in top leadership. "It just seems to me that you could find someone better. More suited to this position," he said. I told him that actually most leaders feel that there could be someone better. But I really believe in him and told him that he is the right man for the job.

In the same way, Moses said to God, "Who am I, that I should go to Pharaoh and bring the Israelites out of Egypt?"

God's answer: I will be with you, and I will give you a sign (v. 12).

EXCUSE #2 — THE EXCUSE OF AUTHORITY

In his second excuse in Exodus 3:13, Moses was convinced that the Israelites would not believe that God sent him. How would he prove to them that he had God's authority? Many leaders struggle with having the authority to lead, because of fuzzy organizational structures and dysfunctional boards. But the struggle is real because of low respect for leaders in general in our culture. Everyone questions leaders, and there is virtually no power distance between leader and follower here in the United States. As I travel to many other parts of the world, I find that this isn't true elsewhere. In Korea, where I recently gave several lectures, the power distance is as great as ever! Moses obviously felt a similar insecurity.

Moses said to God, "Suppose I go to the Israelites and say to them, 'The God of your fathers has sent me to you,' and they ask me, 'What is his name?' Then what shall I tell them?"

God's answer: Tell them "I am" has sent me to you. Tell them that the God of your fathers—the God of Abraham, Isaac, and Jacob—has sent me to you (vv. 14–15).

EXCUSE #3 — THE EXCUSE OF CREDIBILITY

His third excuse in Exodus 4:1 is very similar to the second. Moses still thought that they would not believe he was God's man for this deliverance.

"What if they do not believe me or listen to me and say, 'The LORD did not appear to you?'" he asked God.

God's answer: I'm going to give you all kinds of miraculous powers to show people that I sent you. These will include your miraculous staff and your withered hand.

Sometimes in my own leadership, when my people doubt me, I wish I had one of those magic sticks.

EXCUSE #4—THE EXCUSE OF GIFTING

It appears that Moses believed God up to this point. In Exodus 4:10 Moses turned his excuses inward on his capabilities. He basically told God that he could not be a public speaker. I guess he knew he was going to be doing a lot of speaking, which comes with most leadership positions.

Moses said to the Lord, "O Lord, I have never been eloquent, neither in the past nor since you have spoken to your servant. I am slow of speech and tongue."

God's answer: I made your mouth, and I will teach you what to say.

God's message here is that He will take care of the gifting piece if we allow ourselves to be available and obedient. This is where we need a lot of grace with one another. We all have strengths as leaders, but when the weaknesses come out, we have to bear with each other as we grow into our roles. In the book *The Ascent of a Leader*, Bill Thrall, Bruce McNicol, and Ken McElrath teach the concept that your gifts might get you to the top, but only character can keep you there. Somehow I think that this was exactly what God saw in Moses.

> **THE EXCUSE OF GIFTING**
>
> "MASTER, PLEASE, I DON'T TALK WELL. I'VE NEVER BEEN GOOD WITH WORDS, NEITHER BEFORE NOR AFTER YOU SPOKE TO ME. I STUTTER AND STAMMER" (EX. 4:10 MSG).

Excuse #5—Excuse of Cowardice

Finally, Moses exploded with the mother of all excuses in Exodus 4:13. I've heard it said that all excuses are equal. Moses had run out of excuses, so he just gave up and pleaded with God to send someone else. This is what I call the prayer of the reluctant leader:

"O Lord, please send someone else to do it," Moses begged.

God's answer: At this point God actually got angry with Moses. He appointed Moses' brother, Aaron, to be his mouthpiece. And he reminded Moses to take the miraculous staff with him. In effect God said, "Look, I'm going to work with you whether you like it or not!" (vv. 14–17).

So Why Did God Decide to Use Moses?

> THE FACT THAT MOSES DID NOT FEEL HE HAD ANYTHING TO OFFER MADE HIM PERFECT FOR THE JOB.

Why did God put up with so much reluctance and press ahead? Similarly, how often do you ask yourself why He decided to use you? Moses was an arrogant man in his forties, but by the time God called him through the burning bush, he was a humbled man in his eighties—ready for his assignment. I think God saw in him the right heart for the job—as He did in David—and just had to downsize his ego. Moses' forty years in the desert took care of that problem.

I find it interesting that God got mad at Moses for his excuses but did not fire him: "Then the LORD's anger burned against Moses and he said, 'What about your brother, Aaron the Levite?'" (Ex. 4:14). He could easily have found someone else. But He knew that Moses was the right man for this job.

God cannot use people who are full of themselves. He prefers empty vessels. Why did Jesus choose fishermen to be His inner circle? Same reason. They were not prominent, highly gifted, or wealthy. They were perfect candidates for Jesus to mold into the leaders He needed them to be. My take on God's choice of Moses is that Moses' ego was not going to get in the way. God knew that Moses was up for the selfless task of leading God's people on a very difficult journey. I think a whole lot of very gifted people do not make themselves available to God. So the fact that Moses did not feel he had anything to offer made him perfect for the job.

Do you struggle with feelings of inadequacy? Are you plagued with self-doubts? Do you ever wonder why God chose you to lead your church, ministry, or business? Are you convinced that God could find someone better to lead your organization? Do you ever find that self-doubt crashes over you like ocean waves? You are not alone. In my years of interviewing leaders and training future leaders, I've seen this in one heart after another.

Buck Hatch, my favorite professor in college, is a great example of a weeping leader. I met Donna when I was a student at Columbia International University, in Columbia, South Carolina. Anyone who attended Columbia during the '60s, '70s, or '80s would likely agree that their favorite professor was Buck Hatch. Donna and I enjoyed his classes the most because Buck taught the Bible like no one I've heard before or since. We actually called him "the weeping prophet." He had a sad disposition much like that of Jeremiah in the Old Testament. He dreaded standing before his students, and you could see the pain in his demeanor as he began to talk. He stood hunched over the lectern and often found it hard to lift up his eyes to look at the class.

Underneath his painful demeanor was a fire for God and His Word that captured our hearts. His words were like the best meal you've ever enjoyed. All of a sudden he would say in a strong voice, "Look up here," as he drew the story of the Bible on the board. He had an unusual gift for breaking open the Word of God with clarity and conviction and fascination. A whole generation of students who went to Columbia learned the Bible, sitting at the feet of Buck Hatch. Professor Hatch would often share his inner struggles with us. He told us that he was often depressed and had a gloomy outlook on life. It all went back to his childhood, but he did not want to talk about that. The praise of the faculty and students meant nothing to him. He faithfully fulfilled his teaching duties only out of a sense of obligation to the call of God. I can't help but think that Moses came from the same place of inadequacy.

SEVEN DEADLY MOTIVES

So if being a reluctant leader is a good thing, what's the other side of the coin? What are the wrong reasons to want to lead? None of us have perfectly pure motives in leadership, but there are some dangers to avoid in the struggle to lead out of a pure heart. Men and women the world over and through all of time have been tempted by power, prestige, position, popularity, pride, personal gain, and a nice paycheck. But I always think about the model of David, the man after God's own heart who seemed to have a heart protected from dark motives, at least as it concerned his leadership: "And David shepherded them with integrity of heart; with skillful hands he led them" (Ps. 78:72). He, like Moses, was able to avoid the destructive snares of leadership.

What happens to people who work under leaders with any of these darker motives? It shouldn't be hard to find someone you can ask! The bottom line is that you feel like you are serving them instead of them serving the mission of your organization.

Rick Warren starts his book *The Purpose Driven Life* with this statement: "It's not about you."[1] That single line is a good lesson for leaders in all walks of life! I know this has become a bigger challenge for Rick since the explosion of the popularity of his book. He's become a very wealthy man by writing those words of humility. Isn't that ironic? However, I just heard him say again the other day, "It is still not about me." Rick now reverse tithes, as he and his wife live on 10 percent of their money and give away 90 percent.

In my thirties God accomplished a major rightsizing of my ego. I was a seminary graduate and thought I was God's

THE SEVEN DEADLY MOTIVES FOR LEADERSHIP

POWER
PRESTIGE
POSITION
POPULARITY
PRIDE
PERSONAL GAIN
PAYCHECK

gift to the world. At that time, it really was all about me. I knew it all and could achieve great leadership feats in my own strength—a lot like Moses when he tried to fight for the Israelites and killed the Egyptian and hid him in the sand (Ex. 2). God had to send me to the back side of the desert to deal with my pride. Through some harsh negative feedback from my colleagues, I began to realize that I really was not an instrument that could be used by God for great things. *But I wanted to be.* Through a series of events, God crushed my ego and prepared my heart to be a better leader. And I appreciate that I did not have to spend an entire forty years out in the Arizona desert.

THE POWER OF HUMILITY

As I continue to study the Bible through the years, especially as it relates to leadership, I can't help but notice how many places the issue of humility pops up. Please allow me to finish this chapter with a few of my favorite examples from the New Testament—from Paul to Peter. Like Moses, they, too, learned the power of humility.

> To keep me from becoming conceited because of these surpassingly great revelations, there was given me a thorn in my flesh, a messenger of Satan, to torment me. Three times I pleaded with the Lord to take it away from me. But he said to me, "My grace is sufficient for you, for my power is made perfect

in weakness." Therefore I will boast all the more gladly about my weaknesses, so that Christ's power may rest on me. That is why, for Christ's sake, I delight in weaknesses, in insults, in hardships, in persecutions, in difficulties. For when I am weak, then I am strong. (2 Cor. 12:7–10)

Here is a trustworthy saying that deserves full acceptance: Christ Jesus came into the world to save sinners—of whom I am the worst. But for that very reason I was shown mercy so that in me, the worst of sinners, Christ Jesus might display his unlimited patience as an example for those who would believe on him and receive eternal life. (1 Tim. 1:15–16)

Be completely humble and gentle; be patient, bearing with one another in love. (Eph. 4:2)

Do nothing out of selfish ambition or vain conceit, but in humility consider others better than yourselves. (Phil. 2:3)

Therefore, as God's chosen people, holy and dearly loved, clothe yourselves with compassion, kindness, humility, gentleness and patience. Bear with each other and forgive whatever grievances you may have against one another. Forgive as the Lord forgave you. (Col. 3:12–13)

To the elders among you, I appeal as a fellow elder, a witness of Christ's sufferings and one who also will share in the glory to be revealed: Be shepherds of God's flock that is under your care, serving as overseers—not because you must, but because you are willing, as God wants you to be; not greedy for money, but eager to serve; not lording it over those entrusted to you, but being examples to the flock. And when the Chief Shepherd appears, you will receive the crown of glory that will never fade away. (1 Peter 5:1–4)

3

LEADERSHIP COMMANDMENT #3: THOU SHALT PRACTICE SERVANT LEADERSHIP

The LORD said to Moses: "Bring me seventy of Israel's elders who are known to you as leaders and officials among the people. Have them come to the Tent of Meeting, that they may stand there with you. I will come down and speak with you there, and I will take of the Spirit that is on you and put the Spirit on them. They will help you carry the burden of the people so that you will not have to carry it alone." (Num. 11:16–17)

Big Idea: A servant leader cares more about the good of the
organization and its people than his or her own enrichment.
Servant leaders are not about being self-centered, but
they love to share the load. They are team focused.

The former CEO of British Petroleum, Tony Hayward, became a PR nightmare for his company during the Gulf oil spill in 2010. In the middle of the crisis he was quoted on international television as saying, "I'd like my life back." He also said at the White House in front of rolling cameras, "I want the world to know that BP cares about the little people in the Gulf area." It wasn't long before he had to leave his job in great humiliation. I'm so glad that Moses never said to God, "I just want my life in Egypt back." Nor did he request of Pharaoh, "Let these little people go." Hayward is the opposite of a servant leader and a prime example of a self-centered leader insulated from rank-and-file people in his organization.

> **SERVANT LEADERSHIP:**
>
> **WHEN THE LEADER CARES MORE ABOUT THE GOOD OF THE ORGANIZATION AND ITS PEOPLE THAN HIS OR HER OWN ENRICHMENT.**

Servant leadership—what is it really? My definition of servant leadership is simply: *when the leader cares more about the good of the organization and its people than his or her own enrichment.* That is precisely why I believe, in the end, Moses accepted God's assignment. Moses decided it was more about "we" than it was about "me." If Moses wanted to build up his career and follow his personal dream, he never would've thrown his lot in with the Israelites. The easy road for him would have been to stay in the life of luxury in the palaces of Egypt. He essentially threw away his future when he sided with the Israelites. Moses' sacrifice for God is really crystallized in the book of Hebrews in the New Testament, where the writer summarizes the life of Moses:

> By faith Moses, when he had grown up, refused to
> be known as the son of Pharaoh's daughter. *He chose*
> *to be mistreated along with the people of God* rather
> than to enjoy the pleasures of sin for a short time.
> He regarded disgrace for the sake of Christ as of
> greater value than the treasures of Egypt, because he
> was looking ahead to his reward. (Heb. 11:24–26)

The opposite of *servant leadership* is *self-serving leadership*. And we seem to see a lot of that around us every day in Washington and Wall Street. Here are the primary differences between *servant leadership* and *self-serving leadership*:

Servant Leadership	Self-Serving Leadership
It's all about "we"	It's all about "me"
I serve others	Others serve me
I am happy if the team scores	I'm happy when I score
I carry everyone on my shoulders	I ride on the shoulders of everyone else
The needs of others come first	My needs come first
I am here for our cause	I'm here for my career
I am a shepherd	I am a hired hand
I want to help you fulfill your dreams	I am here to pursue my dreams
Empowerment	Micromanagement
"Let my people go"	"Let me have my way"

LET MY PEOPLE GO

Something happened to Moses during those forty years he spent on the back side of the desert. He went into the desert as an arrogant forty-year-old, and came out bearing humility and greatness. One thing that occurred during those years of tending sheep was his conversion from a self-serving person to a servant leader. As we saw in Hebrews 11, he chose to be identified with the Israelites rather than the Egyptian family that raised him. He bonded with the Israelites. When Moses said to his father in law Jethro in Exodus 4:18, "Let me go back to *my own people* in Egypt to see if any of them are still alive," he had made the transition to servant leadership. Remember that they were not really "his" people! He grew up in Pharaoh's household. He had nothing in common with the Israelites other than his heritage. For all practical purposes Moses had become Egyptian.

Everyone knew Moses as a son of royalty. His mom lived in the White House, and he grew up there. The Egyptians looked down on the Israelites and made them slave laborers for the rich. But after the forty years of processing, he finally realized that they were *his* people and that he belonged with them. He did not say to Pharaoh, "Let these people go." Not, "Let God's people go." Not, "Give these little people a break and free them from slavery so I can get on with my life." No, he said to Pharaoh, "The Lord is saying, 'Let My people go,' and FYI, they are *my* people too."

Many leaders do not feel that they have a lot in common with the people they are charged to lead. Often we get thrown onto teams where the greatest conflict arises from cultural differences. Early in our ministry in Vienna, I remember Donna having a hard time with a woman from the Deep South. Donna was a Chicago girl, and a lot of the ways of this Southern woman grated against her. I often see this conflict occur in churches or businesses where a pastor or leader comes to town from another region of the country. Huge issues can arise from cultural differences. Do you think that people in Oregon think differently from those living in Texas? How about someone from Georgia leading a team in Silicon Valley, California? We may share common values but ...

We are as different as:

Our homes we were raised in

Our parents

Our economic standing growing up

Our extended family

Our hometown and region of the country

Our educational level

Our church background

Our spiritual roots and traditions

Our conversion story and discipleship

Our nationalities

Our ethnicity

Our _____ (fill in the blank).

BOTTOM-UP LEADERSHIP

The image of Charlton Heston standing on the mountain after parting the Red Sea is not exactly the same image of the humble servant leader we read about in the Bible. The Old Testament claims that Moses was the most humble man on earth (Num. 12:3). His years in the wilderness made him so. But how is it that Moses displayed and practiced this humility, and how did it help him in his task? How do we practice being strong leaders while also displaying the humility of Jesus as servant leaders?

I recall years ago speaking to a group of CEOs at a gathering in one of those tall glass buildings in downtown Chicago. They all wore their power suits and came to listen to me speak on leadership.

I unpacked this theme of servant leadership, and they just didn't get it. They told me that to show *any* signs of weakness was death to their careers. I used the example of Jesus, who embodied strength bathed in service to others, but unfortunately, I don't think the concept sunk in.

THE UPSIDE-DOWN ORG CHART

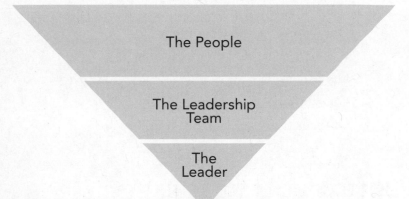

THE SERVANT LEADER CARRIES THE LOAD WITH HIS OR HER TEAM

This organizational diagram illustrates the servant-style leadership of Jesus Christ, as well as the servant-style leadership of Moses. In the inverted pyramid, we find an upside-down approach to leadership, where everything rests on the shoulders of the leader. This leadership style is more of an attitude than anything else, an attitude in which leaders realize that they carry the organization on their shoulders and that their goal is to help make everyone else successful.

As I've grown in my leadership responsibilities, I've come to realize that I bear more and more of the burdens of more and more people.

Recently someone commented to me, "It must feel great to be the leader of such a large organization." I chuckled as I shared with him that in fact it's not what it looks like from the outside. The higher you go in leadership, the more headaches you bear because of other people's problems. The toughest problems get shipped to the person where the buck stops.

I don't care for traditional top-down organization charts. They focus on leaders being at the top and dominating everything (and everyone) below them. In our organization, we developed the flywheel approach to our organization chart. I like it because it shows that the real work happens on the outside of the wheel. We, inside the circles, support their efforts and empower them to be successful.

The Flywheel Org Chart

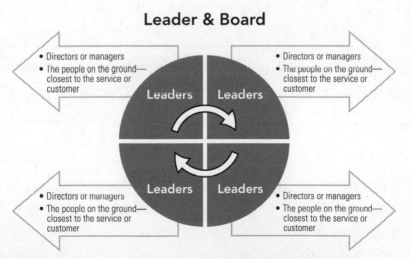

Leader & Board

- Directors or managers
- The people on the ground— closest to the service or customer

- Directors or managers
- The people on the ground— closest to the service or customer

Leaders   Leaders

Leaders   Leaders

- Directors or managers
- The people on the ground— closest to the service or customer

- Directors or managers
- The people on the ground— closest to the service or customer

The Servant Leader Enables
the People to Succeed

Moses developed a strong team around him. He listened when God told him not to go it alone. Similarly, a servant leader staffs to his or her weaknesses. They have enough self-confidence to surround themselves with people more gifted than they are. One key to effective servant leadership is leading with a team and through a team. It is not about "me"; it is about "we." The seventy elders who led with Moses became a powerful team that surrounded him:

> The LORD said to Moses: "Bring me seventy of Israel's elders who are known to you as leaders and officials among the people. Have them come to the Tent of Meeting, that they may stand there with you. I will come down and speak with you there, *and I will take of the Spirit that is on you and put the Spirit on them. They will help you carry the burden of the people so that you will not have to carry it alone."* (Num. 11:16–17)

Hire Stars and Set Them Free

I love hiring strong leaders and setting them free to lead. In fact, I like to stay out of their way. I just hired such a person, and he is shaking things up in a good way that I cannot. I am his champion as he leads in his areas of strength. Recently, he and I and another leader on our team made a list of the strengths that we each bring to the organization. Each of us shared what we saw as the five top contributions or strengths that the others uniquely contributed. I was amazed at the contrast among our lists, and surprisingly, there was little overlap. As we honor those strengths, we see how uniquely each one of us serves the team. I know that these leaders can bring things to the organization that I am not capable of ever bringing.

It is in the verses from Numbers 11 that we begin to see how a leader shares the load. Once we get over ourselves and quit being control freaks, we can begin to let others lead. We lead as a team, not as an island. The key phrase in this message from God to Moses is, *"And I will take of the Spirit that is on you and put the Spirit on them"* (v. 17). I have seen a whole lot of leaders who are *not okay* with sharing the responsibility. But do you realize that Jesus Himself believed in building a team and working through a team? He too had His seventy leaders to share the load and launch His movement:

> The Lord now chose seventy-two other disciples and sent them ahead in pairs to all the towns and places he planned to visit. These were his instructions to them: "The harvest is great, but the workers are few. So pray to the Lord who is in charge of the harvest; ask him to send more workers into his fields." (Luke 10:1–2 NLT)

I love the saying I picked up years ago, which continues to be one of my favorites: "Blessed are the control freaks, for they shall inhibit the earth." But servant leadership is the opposite … even

people out in the marketplace are figuring that out! I love what Herb
Kelleher, the cofounder of Southwest Airlines, says about control:

> A financial analyst once asked me if I was afraid
> of losing control of our organization. I told him
> I've never had control and I never wanted it. If
> you create an environment where the people truly
> participate, you don't *need* control. They know
> what needs to be done, and they do it…. I have
> always believed that the best leader is the best
> server. And if you're a servant, by definition you're
> not controlling.[1]

I love the fact that even leaders in the marketplace are getting
this. It's not new for us who work in the ministry realm. But it's nice
to have the confirmation from top leaders "out there."

Jim Collins is just such an expert on leadership. I devour everything he writes. In his book *How the Mighty Fall,* he shows that
arrogance and the lack of humility are some of the great causes of
corporate failures. In his classic book *Good to Great,* Collins recognized the power of servant leadership. He calls it "Level 5" leadership.
After analyzing hundreds of companies, he observed that the leaders
of the most successful, long-standing, and truly great companies are
Level 5 leaders, who lead through their teams.

Level 5 leaders are humble because they clearly know their own
limitations. Instead of promoting their own visions, they get their
leaders together and pepper them with probing questions to draw
new strategies out of them. Therefore, the essential difference is

that the Level 4 leader provides direction while the Level 5 leader is a facilitator who draws ideas for new directions out of his or her people. Level 5 leadership is really a modern version of the management paradigm known as participative leadership, which has been around for decades.

SHEPHERDS ARE SERVANTS

Recently on a trip to Albania, Donna and I walked every afternoon on the hillsides of Korçë to get some exercise and a break from our speaking schedule. Two days in a row, we could not help but notice a shepherd tending to his flock of sheep. It seems like such a boring job—he meandered after the sheep and kept an eye on them. A lot of his time was spent just standing around, leaning on his staff, and smoking cigarettes (modern shepherds!). Every day it was the same routine. *Man,* I thought, *he must* really *like those sheep to continue doing that job.*

The Bible is filled with analogies comparing leadership to shepherding. Even Jesus is called the Great Shepherd. Hebrews 13:20 reads, "May the God of peace, who through the blood of the eternal covenant brought back from the dead our Lord Jesus, that great Shepherd of the sheep … "

Why did Jesus use the shepherd analogy for leadership? I think He used it because shepherds keep a lifelong commitment to stay with their sheep. It is a life of sacrifice.

In his book *While Shepherds Watch Their Flocks*, Timothy Laniak interviewed shepherds all over the Middle East. In Jordan, he asked a bedouin, "What does it take to be a shepherd?" Sitting in his tent, the shepherd replied, "What really matters is that you have the heart for it."[2]

That, too, is the essence of servant leadership—you must have a *heart* for your people. The prophet Ezekiel warned against shepherds who were not servants:

> Son of man, prophesy against the shepherds of Israel; prophesy and say to them: "This is what the Sovereign LORD says: *Woe to the shepherds of Israel who only take care of themselves!* Should not shepherds take care of the flock? You eat the curds, clothe yourselves with the wool and slaughter the choice animals, but you do not take care of the flock. You have not strengthened the weak or healed the sick or bound up the injured. You have not brought back the strays or searched for the lost. You have ruled them harshly and brutally."
> (Ezek. 34:2–4)

Woe to shepherds like the barons of Wall Street, or the CEOs like Tony Hayward who take care of only themselves. The New Testament is rich with this shepherd analogy. Here are some of my favorite verses, all of which apply the shepherd concept to leadership:

> When he saw the crowds, he had compassion on them, because they were harassed and helpless, like sheep without a shepherd. (Matt. 9:36)

I am the good shepherd. The good shepherd lays down his life for the sheep. (John 10:11)

Keep watch over yourselves and all the flock of which the Holy Spirit has made you overseers. Be shepherds of the church of God, which he bought with his own blood. (Acts 20:28)

Be shepherds of God's flock that is under your care, serving as overseers—not because you must, but because you are willing, as God wants you to be; not greedy for money, but eager to serve. (1 Peter 5:2)

JESUS SHOWS A BETTER WAY

When it comes to servant leadership, there is no better model than that of Jesus Christ. On the night He was betrayed, Jesus showed His followers just how much He loved them. We read in John 13, verse 1, that He "knew that the time had come for him to leave this world and go to the Father. Having loved his own who were in the world, he now showed them the full extent of his love." At that point Jesus gave His final and ultimate demonstration of servant leadership: He washed the disciples' feet!

The foundation for His servanthood was a true realization of His power, position, and prestige. He was God Himself in the flesh and had every right to be a dictator. In fact, He is the only man to walk on the face of the earth who had the right to be an absolute dictator! Jesus deserves to be served.

However, Jesus demonstrated servant leadership by taking off His robe, picking up a towel, and washing His disciples' feet. If I'd been there that night, I would have been embarrassed beyond words the moment I saw Him pick up the towel and begin to wash the first set of feet. But someone had to get up to take care of this necessary chore, and yet no one took the initiative. Jesus demonstrated that he who was to be greatest among His followers would be the servant of all. To me the essence of servant leadership is to take the initiative no matter how menial the task. We should not wait, figuring "someone else" will do the job because it's beneath our pay grade.

> JESUS IS THE ONLY MAN TO WALK ON THE FACE OF THE EARTH WHO HAD THE RIGHT TO BE AN ABSOLUTE DICTATOR!

The explanation of His servant leadership comes at the end of the story, when Jesus says, "I have set you an example that you should do as I have done for you. I tell you the truth, no servant is greater than his master, nor is a messenger greater than the one who sent him. Now that you know these things, you will be blessed if you do them" (John 13:15–17).

The apostle Peter was at the Last Supper that night. In fact, if you recall, he was the one who refused to have his feet washed by Jesus. He objected loudly. But when Jesus told him it was the only way for Peter to be included in Jesus' inner circle, he acquiesced.

Somehow that night Peter got the concept of servant leadership. In 1 Peter, which he would write years later, Peter passed along the same teaching to his followers. This is one of those great servant leadership passages that speak eloquently about how to be a leader in God's economy:

> To the elders among you, I appeal as a fellow elder, a witness of Christ's sufferings and one who also will share in the glory to be revealed: Be shepherds of God's flock that is under your care, serving as overseers—not because you must, but because you are willing, as God wants you to be; not greedy for money, but eager to serve; not lording it over those entrusted to you, but being examples to the flock. And when the Chief Shepherd appears, you will receive the crown of glory that will never fade away.
>
> Young men, in the same way be submissive to those who are older. All of you, clothe yourselves with humility toward one another, because,
>
> "God opposes the proud
> but gives grace to the humble."
>
> Humble yourselves, therefore, under God's mighty hand, that he may lift you up in due time. Cast all your anxiety on him because he cares for you. (1 Peter 5:1–7)

THE SERVANT LEADER'S PRAYER

A servant leader must pray for his or her people. The more frustrated I get with some people, the more I find that I pray for them. If I take the time to talk to God about these people and the problems I'm having, something shifts in my spirit. I guess I start to see them in a different light. This is another lesson I have learned from my mentor Moses.

The selfless nature of Moses came through once again when God presented him with the "second edition" stone tablets. Moses destroyed the first set of the Ten Commandments in anger, when he came down and found the Israelites worshipping the golden calf. I'm not sure what I would have done at that point. Call it a day and find another job? Not Moses. As a good shepherd and servant leader he marched right back up that mountain to receive the second set of stone tablets. In Exodus 34 we read the intimate account of how God came down in a cloud and stood there in the presence of Moses and proclaimed His name. In effect God said, "Although the people don't deserve it, I'm giving them another chance."

Exodus 34:4–7 says this:

> So Moses chiseled out two stone tablets like the first ones and went up Mount Sinai early in the morning, as the LORD had commanded him; and he carried the two stone tablets in his hands. Then the LORD came down in the cloud and stood there with him and proclaimed his name, the LORD. And he passed in front of Moses, proclaiming, "The

LORD, the LORD, the compassionate and gracious
God, slow to anger, abounding in love and faithfulness, maintaining love to thousands, and forgiving
wickedness, rebellion and sin."

At this moment Moses bowed down to the ground and worshipped God. He prayed what I would call *the ultimate prayer of a
servant leader*. He begged God to go with them. Moses acknowl-
edged how corrupt the people were—"Yes, we deserve to be toast.
I'm actually astonished that we're still alive and talking to You."
He identified with his people even though he was absent when
they sinned. Then Moses pleads with God to "take us as your
inheritance."

The prayer of a servant leader:

Moses bowed to the ground at once and worshiped.
"O Lord, if I have found favor in your eyes," he
said, "then let the Lord go with us. Although this
is a stiff-necked people, forgive our wickedness
and our sin, and take us as your inheritance." (Ex.
34:8–9)

4

LEADERSHIP COMMANDMENT #4: THOU SHALT BE OPPOSED, RESISTED, AND MISUNDERSTOOD

They said to Moses, "Was it because there were no graves in Egypt that you brought us to the desert to die? What have you done to us by bringing us out of Egypt? Didn't we say to you in Egypt, 'Leave us alone; let us serve the Egyptians'? It would have been better for us to serve the Egyptians than to die in the desert!" (Ex. 14:11–12)

Big Idea: Great leaders face great opposition. The bigger the vision, the more some people will resist it. Expect opposition, and learn how to deal with it when it comes.

"Being responsible sometimes means p***ing people off," observed military leader Colin Powell. He said it, not me, but I agree with him. Great leaders face great opposition.

Just about everyone rebelled against Moses' leadership sooner or later. The rank-and-file followers did not respect him, his closest aides rebelled, and even his friends and family turned against him. There are no wounds more painful than wounds from those closest to us. However, Robert Jarvik, inventor of the artificial heart, observed, "Leaders are visionaries with a poorly developed sense of fear and no concept of the odds against them."

CONFLICT BETWEEN PEOPLE ALWAYS ARISES WHEN THERE'S A SIGNIFICANT DIFFERENCE IN EXPECTATIONS.

Sometimes the pressure of leadership is overwhelming to me. In fact, this week I'm having one of those weeks. I went home from the office the night before last feeling so discouraged that I wanted to quit. I didn't want to talk to Donna about it, so I just allowed some criticism I received in a meeting at the office to churn inside. I am a master at internalizing criticism, and I went to sleep so upset that I tossed and turned all night. I rehearsed in my mind the unfair things that were said about me and how I would answer my critics as soon as I was given the chance. Sometimes I am criticized because of my decisions, but this time it was related to my apparent inaction. When we don't do what people expect us to do, they can get frustrated with our leadership. It's an issue of differing expectations. When Moses lingered on the mountain for forty days, his followers grew impatient with his leadership: "He is not really fulfilling our expectations. Our leader is AWOL!"

Conflict between people always arises when there's a significant difference in expectations. I disappoint some people by what I am *not* as a leader, and similarly, you will disappoint some people by what you're not. This is simply part of what leadership is about. This week I feel overwhelmed by the expectations of what others think I should be doing with my time and how I should be fulfilling their agendas. But getting defensive is not the answer. What I learned *again* this week is that as a leader I cannot subsist on the fuel of appreciation from others. It's not my job to please people. I decided a long time ago that I can please some of the people some of the time, but never all of the people all of the time! But as much as I know leadership is not a popularity contest and it is not about pleasing people—I do want them to like me. I can't help it.

Have you ever noticed that everyone thinks he or she knows how you should do your job? Colin Powell is unfortunately right—sometimes if we do the right thing, people get mad. This is not about being

> NOT ONLY DID MOSES DEAL WITH BETRAYAL, BUT HE ALSO LED A GROUP OF FOLLOWERS WHO HAD MASTERED THE FINE ART OF WHINING.

a good politician; it's about counting on resistance and being prepared to handle it rightly before God. Not only did Moses deal with betrayal, but he also led a group of followers who had mastered the fine art of whining. His fickle followers were enthusiastic one day and despondent the next. One day he was their hero and the next day the villain. Sometimes we will have to lead people who would not be our first-choice candidates. Face it: Many times we do not choose our followers, and they do not choose us. But how did Moses respond to his fickle followers? What lessons can we learn from Moses about how to deal with whining—or worse, betrayal?

The first lesson I learned from Moses is that we have to play the cards we are dealt—and lead the people God asks us to lead. Most leaders don't get to choose their followers and have to live with some kind of resistance at every turn. How did you get into your current leadership assignment? Did your boss hire you? Did you volunteer? Most leaders I know are hired, appointed, or elected by some kind of governing body, board, or leader. The owner, the chairman, the church elders, the nonprofit board of directors, or a management group of some kind often selects the leaders in an organization. Many times there is a search committee involved. That is what happened to me.

In my case, the decision rested fully with the board with no voting by the followers. When they chose me, I was shocked, and many others on the team in those days were equally surprised. I was not the likely heir apparent. I wonder how many of the Israelites felt that way about Moses and his leadership. We know they felt that way in the beginning: "The man said, 'Who made you ruler and judge over us?'" (Ex. 2:14a). They were essentially saying to God, "This is the best you've got? Why don't you let us have an election?"

Once you assume a leadership position, you are often thrust upon the followers, and they have to get to know you. Some will like you, and some won't. You have to start by earning their trust. Some will have an easy time following your lead, but there will always be the few who just don't care for you. Sometimes it's just a matter of poor chemistry.

I have seen through the years that it's impossible to have great chemistry with everybody in your organization. I can think right now of a couple of people I have worked with for years whom I highly respect but with whom I have strained chemistry. We just don't enjoy one another's presence. It is awkward and forced, and we never seem to see things the same way. Here is the chemistry test: Would you invite this person to go grab coffee with you and just hang out at Starbucks? Can you be yourself unscripted? I can guarantee that if you sense bad chemistry with some people in your organization, it is probably a two-way street, and they likely feel the same about you. In my case, despite the lack of great chemistry with these people, I still value their contribution to the team, and I know that teams can work even with some poor personal chemistry. At the same time, I couldn't have people like that on my direct report leadership team—people I work with day in and day out.

Sometimes the few resisters can hold back the many. When it comes to opposition, I've seen some crazy things happen in business and nonprofit work, but especially in local churches. I have seen some leaders hamstrung by a small handful of resisters. Churches can be the worst in this regard, because pastors are too kind to deal with the people who act as human roadblocks. We suffer from *terminal niceness*. We think that Christ followers should not fire other Christ followers. And how can you fire people in a congregation? I have a pastor friend who told me of three families that have held his church hostage with their continual resistance. No one has the courage to stand up to them, so through their resistance these people have run

the church for *decades*. As a result the church is entangled in the cob-
webs of the past. Many organizations and businesses also have these
informal gatekeepers who tie the group to the past and powerfully
resist any attempts to radically change things.

Donna and I watched this play out painfully and personally
in our first ministry experience after seminary. I went to work for
my father-in-law, who was the senior pastor of a church in Long
Beach, California. He was the new pastor trying to lead a group of
laypeople who had been in this church for over thirty years. I would
describe it as a country-club church, as there was a lot of fellowship
but not a whole lot of spirituality. It was a comfortable congregation,
but the membership was slowly declining. There were a handful of
families that had pretty well controlled the church *and* the pastor
through the years. It wasn't long before they decided they did not like
my father-in-law, who was just too spiritual for them. He preached
sermons and launched initiatives that annoyed the old guard. Long
story short—they maneuvered to have him ousted as their pastor.
Life isn't fair on this side of eternity, and a lot of good people lose
their leadership positions because of carnal opposition.

We did not think that this small group of resisters would win.
God would not allow that. We prayed so much against their plan.
But they did win, and Dad was voted out of the church. The first
big lesson we learned was that life is not fair and that bad things
can happen to really good people. But an even greater lesson Donna
and I learned through that experience was how to respond to unfair
attack. My father-in-law truly responded the way Jesus did when He
was crucified. Dad never once complained to us about the people
who lambasted him. I remember the night that he was voted out of

the church. He told us, "God has something better for me. I have to accept this as His will. Obviously I am no longer to lead this group of people."

The strange postscript to this story is that they asked me to become the pastor after they kicked out my father-in-law. Whereas the chemistry with him was bad, for some reason they really liked my leadership. Of course I did not want to consider the job. But my father-in-law asked me to accept the job for the sake of the church and for the sake of all the good people there. I did so and stayed for two years until Donna and I moved overseas with WorldVenture, the ministry I lead to this day. I admire Donna for being willing to go to church week after week and face the people who had crucified her dad. I am married to an amazing woman!

THE FINE ART OF RESISTING LEADERS

There are many creative ways for people to oppose and resist your leadership. It's not usually as open and confrontational as the story I just shared. Here's the kind of behavior that routinely undermines leadership:

> Passive-aggressive behavior
> Rebellion—subtle or outright
> Disrespect
> Blocking mechanisms
> Side chatter and gossip
> The meeting after the meeting

Spreading rumors

Grumbling (see definition in the following pages)

Subtle undermining

Character assassinations

Paying no attention to leaders

There's a big difference between questioning leaders in a healthy way and the destructive nature of the above list. It's only natural for followers to doubt their leaders. Personally, I always prefer it if people come to me personally with their concerns. I am a very direct person in my dealings with people. But not everyone is like me, and as the boss, I do know that many people are intimidated to speak the truth to me, even in love, and especially in person. I honestly believe I am a good listener. I have learned to embrace doubt, not to shut it down. A good leader will listen to doubt and address people's questions and concerns. The day after I came home so discouraged, I went to the source of the negative feedback and had a very healthy conversation about it. The conversation made me feel much better, and the person gained some valuable insight. I slept much better that night because I felt that at least I was understood and not misrepresented.

MOSES RIDES THE LEADERSHIP ROLLER COASTER

Moses faced the roller coaster of good days and bad days. In fact, if you read Exodus 15 you can see how he goes from the mountaintop of praise to the valley of despair in one fast chapter. In chapter 14, the Israelites saw the great power that God displayed against the Egyptians and they "feared the LORD and put their trust in him and in Moses his servant" (v. 31). The day started off great for Moses. The people were one with God and trusted their leader fully. But by the end of chapter 15 they are complaining and grumbling against Moses, saying, "What are we to drink?" (v. 24). In Exodus 16 they complain that they don't have anything to eat: "The Israelites said to them, 'If only we had died by the LORD's hand in Egypt! There we sat around pots of meat and ate all the food we wanted, but you have brought us out into this desert to starve this entire assembly to death'" (v. 3). First the drinks, then the food! Moses found himself running a community cafeteria.

> IF YOU READ EXODUS 15, YOU CAN SEE HOW MOSES GOES FROM THE MOUNTAINTOP OF PRAISE TO THE VALLEY OF DESPAIR IN ONE FAST CHAPTER.

Things went south in an instant, just like it can for us. One call, email, text message, or meeting—and boom! But God in His graciousness showed up and provided an answer for Moses. Miraculously, it started to rain down bread from heaven in the form of manna. Now manna was not the greatest stuff in the world, but it was nutritious and it filled them up. The definition itself tells you something about this unusual food from heaven: The word *manna* is derived from the Hebrew words meaning "*what is it?*" And that is exactly what the Israelites said when they first saw it! Now part of the deal with manna was that God told them they were allowed to gather only enough for one day. Moses specifically instructed them, "No one is to keep any of it until morning" (Ex. 16:19). So here you go with some great followership: "However, *some of them paid no attention to Moses;* they kept part of it until morning, but it was full of maggots and began to smell. So Moses was angry with them" (v. 20).

Leadership can be a constant emotional roller coaster. One day you're making progress, good things are happening, and then zing! If this is your experience, then you're living in the land of normal. If this is not your experience, then either you're living in isolation and are out of touch with the people, or you haven't been leading long enough yet.

THE ANATOMY OF FOLLOWERS

I love analyzing how followers behave. I've observed that there is always a small group pushing me to be more innovative. These are the early adopters and mavericks who love change and innovation. For this group, we cannot change fast enough! There's also that big block of people in the middle who will follow once they're convinced. You might call them fence sitters. They will sit on the fence and wait to see what happens. There's also a small group that is against everything; I call them "C.A.V.E. People"—they are the Committee Against Virtually Everything. Like the people who ignored the instructions of Moses, they just go about their way, disregarding whatever it is that leadership is trying to do. I've come to conclude that most people fall into one of these three categories when it comes to following the vision of their leaders. I call it the 15-70-15 Principle:

THE FOLLOWERS CONTINUUM

15 Percent Resisters	70 Percent Wait and See	15 Percent Innovators

15 PERCENT: INNOVATORS AND EARLY ADOPTERS

Build on them. They are the foundation for your inner circle of change. They form the idea bank from which you can harvest for your change strategies. They help you cook up the future, and these people are the first to get on board. Treat them well and care for them, because they are going to be there for you when you need them.

70 PERCENT: WAIT AND SEE WHAT HAPPENS

This is the silent majority. These are the people from Missouri: "Show me." Be patient with the silent majority. There is nothing wrong with following the crowd. The great majority of your people will support change once they have been convinced and, more importantly, when they see that others have gone before them.

15 PERCENT: RESISTERS — THE CONVINCED OPPOSITION

Is it unfair to say that you should not waste much time and effort on these people? They can be relics of yesterday who tend to live life with their heads in the sand, away from the action, or perhaps they are simply entrenched, immovable, and unable to change. At times we need to ask them to get off the bus. It's a brutal tactic, but often worth considering. In his book *Good to Great,* Jim Collins makes a big point about getting the right people on the bus and the wrong people off the bus.[1] Sometimes housekeeping has to be done—even a family member or a close friend has to go.

So who do we hear from most when we are up to our eyeballs in leading people through big challenges? The happy middle? The excited innovators? Nope—we hear from the resistance. Who stands up in the business meeting and voices the loudest opinions? The naysayers. But we cannot allow the vocal minority to dominate the desired direction of the convinced majority. I am always amazed at how quiet my fans can be, and at times I have to ask them to speak up for what we are trying to accomplish. I just this week learned that a CEO friend of mine is under attack by a group of international staff that is circulating a petition against his new ideas. They do not like the direction he has taken them—so they have begun a campaign of subversion. I can guarantee that they arise from this small 15 percent. Where are his faithful, loyal 85 percent who are satisfied? Silent.

> WE CANNOT ALLOW THE VOCAL MINORITY TO DOMINATE THE DESIRED DIRECTION OF THE CONVINCED MAJORITY.

MOSES AND HIS FICKLE FOLLOWERS

Moses had some tough moments of opposition in his leadership journey. Sometimes that small group of resisters swayed the 70 percent majority to follow them. Reading these stories is such an encouragement to me. Moses was plagued with what I call fickle followers. They displayed every aspect of the dark side of humanity.

These people caused Moses to cry out to God: "What am I to do with these people? They are almost ready to stone me" (Ex. 17:4).

Actually, I think I have the privilege of leading much better people than he did. I've certainly never seen the degree of rebellion that Moses faced. But the message I see in these stories is to keep faithfully leading the people God has asked me to lead. Love them, forgive them, be patient with them, and treat them as a shepherd treats his sheep.

FIRST SIGNS OF TROUBLE — TRYING TO LEAVE EGYPT

Things were bad from the beginning. Even though God told Moses that Pharaoh would let the people go, it wasn't as easy as Moses thought it would be. Isn't it funny how that happens with all great plans? Instead of letting the people go, Pharaoh made life considerably harder for them by telling them they had to make bricks *without straw*. So the people concluded they were much better off before Moses ever showed up with his wild ideas: "When they left Pharaoh, they found Moses and Aaron waiting to meet them, and they said, 'May the LORD look upon you and judge you! You have made us a stench to Pharaoh and his officials and have put a sword in their hand to kill us'" (Ex. 5:20–21).

SECOND BIG CRISIS — AS THEY LEFT EGYPT

This is when the people told their leader: "Leave us alone!" The Israelites were finally released from slavery and were on their way out of Egypt. As they reached the Red Sea and looked into their rearview mirrors, they saw Pharaoh and his armies approaching. The people were terrified. They were trapped. They were afraid, and they got angry with their leaders. This had to hurt Moses. Can you imagine after all he'd been through that this was the thanks he got? He'd been through his forty years of training, he'd fought for the people, and he'd given them the words of God, *but they just didn't get it:* "They said to Moses, 'Was it because there were no graves in Egypt that you brought us to the desert to die? What have you done to us by bringing us out of Egypt? Didn't we say to you in Egypt, "Leave us alone; let us serve the Egyptians"? It would have been better for us to serve the Egyptians than to die in the desert!'" (Ex. 14:11–12).

GRUMBLING IS OFTEN REALLY AGAINST GOD

It becomes clear in this story of manna and quail coming from heaven that the people were in fact grumbling against God. What a great lesson for leaders in spiritual ministry! If we really believe we're doing God's will and the people resist us, could it be that they are simply fighting obedience to Him? We have to be careful with this and not take it too far. I've seen spiritual dictators go way overboard on pushing "God's will" on the people. But it's also true that there is a rebellion against obedience to God in every human heart. Moses figured it out and made it clear that they were grumbling against God:

> So Moses and Aaron said to all the Israelites, "In
> the evening you will know that it was the LORD
> who brought you out of Egypt, and in the morning

you will see the glory of the LORD, because *he has heard your grumbling against him.* Who are we, that you should grumble against us?" Moses also said, "You will know that it was the LORD when he gives you meat to eat in the evening and all the bread you want in the morning, because he has heard your grumbling against him. Who are we? *You are not grumbling against us, but against the LORD.*" (Ex. 16:6–8)

REPEATED UPS AND DOWNS OF GRUMBLING

The definition of *grumble* is "a complaint uttered in a low and indistinct tone; a low, dull continuous noise; to make complaining remarks or noises under one's breath. To show one's unhappiness or critical attitude."[2]

It appears that some of the Israelites were professional grumblers, and I've met more than a few in my journey. For grumblers, everything is seen through skeptic lenses of scarcity. My wife calls them Eeyores, in reference to the whiny friend of Winnie-the-Pooh. In Exodus 17, when they were camping at Rephidim, they showed their talent again. There was no water for the people to drink. So they quarreled with Moses and said, "Give us water to drink." This was one of those moments of great despair for Moses. And it's a good lesson on how to cope. In moments like these he would cry out to God in desperation. Here's the lesson in that: *When we're at the end of ourselves, God can show up.* I am always tempted to try harder to fix people problems with my own solutions. But I have learned to be quicker about crying out to God for His wisdom, as Moses did:

> But the people were thirsty for water there, and they grumbled against Moses. They said, "Why did you bring us up out of Egypt to make us and our children and livestock die of thirst?"
>
> *Then Moses cried out to the LORD,* "What am I to do with these people? They are almost ready to stone me." (Ex. 17:3–4)

DISAPPOINTING DISOBEDIENCE WITH THE GOLDEN CALF

This is the most famous of all stories of rebellion in the Old Testament. The people grew impatient waiting on Moses, so they devised their own plan. Boy, does that sound familiar. I know that at times, my people grow impatient with the pace of my leadership. If they don't like our plans, they are quick to devise their own. Of course Moses was up on the mountain for forty days, getting his instructions from God. The people knew that but lost faith in the middle of the process. It reminds me of people growing weary in the middle of a long change program or another ambitious or difficult project. The time of greatest volatility among your followers is right there in the middle:

> When the people saw that Moses was so long in coming down from the mountain, they gathered around Aaron and said, "Come, make us gods who

will go before us. As for this fellow Moses who brought us up out of Egypt, *we don't know what has happened to him.*" ...

The L ORD said to Moses ... "They have been quick to turn away from what I commanded them and have made themselves an idol cast in the shape of a calf. They have bowed down to it and sacrificed to it and have said, 'These are your gods, O Israel, who brought you up out of Egypt.'

"I have seen these people," the L ORD said to Moses, "and they are a stiff-necked people." (Ex. 32:1, 7–9)

EVEN HIS CLOSEST FRIENDS TURN ON HIM

Nothing is more painful than the wounds caused by a friend. It's hard to believe that Aaron and Miriam rebelled against the leadership of Moses. You remember that Aaron was the brother of Moses and his close confidant and spokesperson, and Miriam was Moses' sister. We first saw her as a young girl in the book of Exodus. She kept an eye on baby Moses as he floated down the Nile River. We next find Miriam as an adult. In Exodus 15:20–21, she was given the gift of prophecy. She also sang a victory song after the children of Israel crossed the Red Sea. And yet they both turned against Moses in Numbers 12: "Miriam and Aaron began to talk against Moses because of his Cushite wife, for he had married a Cushite. 'Has the L ORD spoken only through Moses?' they asked. 'Hasn't he also spoken through us?' And the L ORD heard this" (Num. 12:1–2).

The conflict arose because of a clash of values. They didn't believe that Moses should have married a Cushite woman. As I already mentioned, it seems that differences in expectations set up so much of the conflict that happened in Moses' journey and conflict that happens on leadership teams. Along with differences in expectations come dramatic differences in values. How we spend money, what we do on vacation, what kind of house we live in, and what sort of car we drive. It can all lead to loss of respect for leadership, which sets up the rebellion. That's what happened in this story. If people go against your leadership, you may need to dig down for the story behind the story. If people are willing to be honest with you, you might discover an underlying clash of expectations and values. And in our culture this kind of criticism comes quickly and often. I like the way God takes the Israelites out to the woodshed and clarifies the authority of Moses: "Why then were you not afraid to speak against my servant Moses?" (Num. 12:8).

How Bad Can It Get? Try Korah's Rebellion

Okay, this one is really bad. In the case of Korah's rebellion, a man named Korah rallied 250 well-known community leaders to rebel against the leadership of Moses and Aaron. How would you handle this kind of opposition if you were in Moses' shoes? I fear that opposition like this would have taken me out. Either way, these men came as a group to oppose Moses and Aaron. Korah and company were fed up with their leadership:

> A CHANGE IMPOSED IS A
> CHANGE OPPOSED.
> —SPENCER JOHNSON,
> WHO MOVED MY CHEESE?

Korah son of Izhar, the son of Kohath, the son of Levi, and certain Reubenites—Dathan and Abiram, sons of Eliab, and On son of Peleth—became insolent and rose up against Moses. With them were 250 Israelite men, well-known community leaders who had been appointed members of the council. *They came as a group to oppose Moses and Aaron and said to them, "You have gone too far!* The whole community is holy, every one of them, and the LORD is with them. Why then do you set yourselves above the LORD's assembly?" (Num. 16:1–3)

The anger at their leaders was white hot. It boiled over. The definition of insolent is "showing a rude or arrogant lack of respect,"[3] so they were ready to vote these two guys off the island for good! This is the old argument: "Who appointed you our leader? What makes you so special?" In the case of Moses, the fact that God appointed him should never have been questioned. As a result, this rebellion really hurt Moses. Numbers 16:4 says, "When Moses heard this, he fell facedown." I can relate to that. When I hear reports of people questioning my leadership actions either directly or indirectly, it devastates me. It is not that I have a need to be right—rather, I just hate being misunderstood. In a recent 360-degree performance review of my leadership, I did not score well with a number of my key peer leadership. This result crushed my spirit because I felt ganged up on and misunderstood. I fully understand why Moses' first reaction to this opposition was to fall facedown. I wonder if he kept saying to God, "See, I told You I was not the right man for this job!" If you want to read how he dealt with the rebellion, read the rest of Numbers 16.

Moses Flunked His 360-Degree Performance Evaluation

Would Moses have passed a 360-degree peer evaluation? I doubt it. Imagine if they had hired a consultant and lined up the anonymous feedback of Aaron, Miriam, Korah, and the 250 elders who rebelled against him. In Numbers 14:4, the leaders said to each other, "We should choose a leader and go back to Egypt." Meaning: "We reject Moses. He is fired, in our book." Notice that they said this "*to each other*," out of the earshot of Moses. It was the meeting after the meeting. Moses was not the leader in these circumstances who garnered warm, fuzzy, positive feedback. He would have utterly failed his professional performance evaluation. He gave them what they needed in his leadership, not what they wanted.

I am all in favor of performance reviews, but not those that are anonymous. I have come to the conviction that the popular practice of anonymous 360-degree peer evaluations is not very biblical. I also see that it seems to do more harm than good to organizations. I have watched friends and colleagues wrongly tortured by this process. My own experience was painful indeed—made more painful by the secretiveness. Very little good has come out of the 360-degree reviews that I have watched up close or at a distance. They end up being more punitive than developmental.

In case you are not familiar with this process, Wikipedia defines 360-degree feedback as "feedback that comes from all around an employee. '360' refers to the 360 degrees in a circle, with an individual

figuratively in the center of the circle. Feedback is provided by subordinates, peers, and supervisors. It also includes a self-assessment
and, in some cases, feedback from external sources such as customers
and suppliers or other interested stakeholders."[4] And in most cases,
the feedback around the circle is anonymous. The theory is that the
anonymous feature will create more accuracy and truth telling.

The consultant who presented the results of my 360 evaluation
took me to a closed-door private session over a full morning. There,
with the magic of PowerPoint, my leadership was laid bare before
my eyes—the good, the bad, and the painful. In the end, I related
to David in Psalm 55, when he felt betrayed by those who worked
closely with him. It is one thing to be attacked by strangers or outsid-
ers, but how about those closest to you? It was not that I felt that
there was gross error; I just felt very alone and ganged up on. I could
not know who said what—all I did hear was a chorus of complaints
hidden behind the anonymous mask. No one had to own his or
her input. Their feedback was reported in secret to the third-party
consultant or plugged into an anonymous Web survey.

I honestly believe that people amp up their courage to be overly
critical because of their ability to hide and not own their words. It is
truth telling gone out of control without accountability. I have seen
leaders ganged up on by subordinates in this secret process behind
closed doors. "He won't know who said what, so here is my chance
to settle that score with my leader!" Do people really do that? I am
afraid that even in the church and in ministry they do. In Korah's
rebellion, at least Moses got the straight scoop face-to-face.

David cried out in Psalm 55:6, "I said, 'Oh, that I had the wings
of a dove! I would fly away and be at rest.'" That was my first reaction

when I heard the negative feedback from my own peers about how I was doing as their leader—flight. These are the people I work with side by side every day. Very little of what I heard had been said to my face.

> If an enemy were insulting me,
>   I could endure it;
> if a foe were raising himself against me,
>   I could hide from him.
> But it is you, a man like myself,
>   my companion, my close friend,
> with whom I once enjoyed sweet fellowship
>   as we walked with the throng at the house of God. (Ps. 55:12–14)

It is this issue of confidentiality and anonymity of the 360 review process that I have the problem with. It flies in the face of the importance of genuine face-to-face conflict resolution. The Bible exhorts us in Ephesians 4:15 to "[speak] the truth in love" to one another as we grow into maturity as a group. I assume that means face-to-face, don't you? I have the right to hear the truth of how you think I am doing as your leader. And you have an obligation to give that feedback in a straightforward way as coming from your mouth. Even if you give the feedback to a third party as part of an evaluation process (i.e., a board of directors), your name should be included with your comments.

Sometimes we in the Christian community seem to be the worst conflict avoiders. We are masters at passive-aggressive behavior. Since we are "the body of Christ," we play nice on the outside. I call it terminal niceness. People are supposed to behave in the church. Christians of all people are *supposed* to love one another. But behind closed doors, we love to criticize as we go septic. We become masters of the meeting after the meeting, when we chew up our leaders. Is it possible that we do it for the sake of maintaining the outward appearance of spirituality? The poison of the tongue was obviously a problem even in the early church, as we read in James 3:7–10: "All kinds of animals, birds, reptiles and creatures of the sea are being tamed and have been tamed by man, but no man can tame the tongue. It is a restless evil, full of deadly poison. With the tongue we praise our Lord and Father, and with it we curse men, who have been made in God's likeness. Out of the same mouth come praise and cursing. My brothers, this should not be."

Jesus instructed us in Matthew 18:15–16, "If a fellow believer hurts you, go and tell him—work it out between the two of you. If he listens, you've made a friend. If he won't listen, take one or two others along so that the presence of witnesses will keep things honest, and try again" (MSG). This passage is addressing the problem of sinning against one another. Many times people have a sense that their leaders sinned against them by the way they treated them or the actions they took. Jesus warned us to work it out face-to-face. If your leader has sinned against you, take it up with him or her face-to-face. If you are afraid to go alone, take someone with you.

In all fairness, my 360-degree review process did help me. As usual, I learned more from pain than from ease and comfort. I learned about the negative way I was coming across to some of my followers. Perception is reality to them whether I like it or not. I learned that I had obviously not listened hard enough or asked enough questions about how I was doing as their leader. And I saw clearly where I need to grow as a leader. Though painful, the 360-degree surgery achieved a new degree of health for me as a leader, though I would not recommend it to others. There are much better ways to accomplish performance reviews that avoid the behind-closed-doors secretiveness.

WHY DO THEY RESIST AND OPPOSE?

So here's the lesson on leadership from the experience of Moses: You will be opposed, resisted, and misunderstood. And if you are naturally a people pleaser, you are in for a rough ride. There will be times when people will grumble against your leadership. Grumbling is not spiritual and can be a deadly disease in an organization, but all leaders have to deal with it. No matter how right you might be, that will not stop the opposition from grumbling.

I have led some big changes in our organization over the years—too many to list. Two of the biggest changes we faced include relocating our offices and changing the name of the organization. Our relocation meant a move of our offices and many families from Chicago to Denver. Not only did we move, but we built a brand-new office building in the middle of the process. The other big change was our name change in 2005. I think

> YOU WILL BE OPPOSED, RESISTED, AND MISUNDERSTOOD. AND IF YOU ARE NATURALLY A PEOPLE PLEASER, YOU ARE IN FOR A ROUGH RIDE.

the relocation and construction of our international headquarters were a much bigger task for me to lead, but I faced much more resistance with the name change. One was about raising money, moving trucks, finding new homes and bricks and mortar, while the other had to do with values and branding. A lot of people have vested interest in the old names of things, no matter how archaic those things might be.

Today we lead people in very different ways than Moses did out in the desert of Sinai. But there are similarities. Much of leadership is about taking people to an uncertain future. Leaders are change agents. Change must always overcome many detractors. And why do people resist change? Well, I have tried to put myself in the shoes of those who followed Moses and create a top ten list—and just about all of these apply to his people. They gave him a hard time because they were human, and it is human nature to resist leaving the old and setting out for the new. Resisting change really boils down to one word: FEAR—"False Expectations Appearing Real."

Top Ten Fears of Change

Fear of the unknown

Fear of loss or failure

Insecurity—I may be worse off

Power—I may lose some

Uncertainty and confusion—misunderstanding
the intent of the change

Inertia—the status quo is strong

Energy and pressure—it takes more work and
stresses us out

Money—it costs more to change things

Lack of trust—our leaders messed up before

Doubt—not sure this is the right direction to solve our
problems

HOW TO DIFFUSE ATTACKS

Finally, let me finish this chapter with some helpful tips for how to handle those attacks *when they come.* I've had some great mentors on this topic through the years. Their advice has proved so valuable when I have faced criticism and opposition to my leadership.

I studied for my doctorate in leadership at Fuller School of Intercultural Studies under the great mentorship of Dr. Bobby Clinton. I studied under Dr. Clinton during a time when I'd been wounded by some hurtful criticism I received early in my career. He taught me a hugely valuable lesson about criticism during that time, and I've tried to apply it over the years. He told me, "Hans, even if they are 95 percent wrong, look for that 5 percent of truth in what they are saying. What is God trying to tell you about your leadership through this criticism? How can you be a better leader through this?" In the years since, I've found that sometimes there's more than just 5 percent truth in criticism, and there is always a message of help for my leadership. In my 360-degree review process, I looked for the more than 5 percent corrective truth in what my peers said about me. And I have honestly worked on self-improvement in the months since that experience. Dr. Clinton was right, and it was through that growing experience that my ego downsized a few notches.

The second great piece of advice came from Ken Williams, who served with Wycliffe Bible Translators as a counselor and trainer and now is a part of Relationship Resources Inc. He developed ten ways to diffuse attacks in the right way. Ken has spent much of his career working with and counseling missionaries, who seem to have a lot of conflict with one another. Here is his list, which I have tried to practice diligently over the years:

Ten Biblical Ways to Defuse an Attack
by Ken Williams, PhD

Keep Silent for Starters (John 19:9; Prov. 17:27–28; Isa. 53:7)

Think Before You React (Prov. 15:28; 29:20; James
    1:19–20)

Really Listen (Prov. 18:2–23; 19:20; James 1:19)

Respond Gently (Prov. 15:1; 16:21; 25:15)

Agree (Matt. 5:25; John 18:37)

  –with whatever is true

  –in principle

  –with the possibility of truth

Give Caring Feedback (John 19:11; Prov. 15:1)

Ask Me for More Clarification (John 18:34; Matt. 5:39–41)

Avoid Quarreling (Eph. 4:31; Prov. 17:14)

Offer to Help (Matt. 5:40–41; Luke 6:27–28)

Ask for Forgiveness, If Appropriate (1 Sam. 15:24–30;
      25:28)[5]

Then finally, having said all I have about resistance and criticism, I want to end this chapter with the wise words of Abraham Lincoln. During his presidency, he was one of the most criticized leaders in American history. However, today there are many statues and monuments built to honor this great leader, but not one erected to honor any of his critics. Sometimes being a good leader is going to upset people. That is part of leadership, and paying too much attention to the critics can *de*mobilize us:

> If I were to try to read, much less answer, all the attacks made on me, this shop might as well be closed for any other business. I do the very best I know how—the very best I can; and I mean to keep on doing so to the end. If the end brings me out all right, what is said against me will not amount to anything. If the end brings me out wrong, ten angels swearing I was right would make no difference.[6]

5

LEADERSHIP COMMANDMENT #5: THOU SHALT HAVE A LIFE

When his father-in-law saw all that Moses was doing for the
people, he said, "What is this you are doing for the people?
Why do you alone sit as judge, while all these people stand
around you from morning till evening?" … Moses' father-in-law
replied, "What you are doing is not good." (Ex. 18:14, 17)

Big Idea: Don't let work trump family. Because of the intense
demands on leaders, it is tempting to get out of balance in
our personal lives. Many leaders fail in their professional
lives because they lose control of their personal lives.

I rode my bike again today, and it was pure therapy. The more
intense my life gets, the more I enjoy riding my bicycle. I guess I'm

not alone because biking is booming in America. Some people might wonder when they see me disappear during the day to hit the trails near my office, "How can he go ride for ninety minutes with all he has to do?" My reaction? How can I not? I work hard. I play hard. The more pressure I have in my work, the more I need the outlet of physical movement. That is a lifestyle commitment I have kept for decades. It helps me cope with leadership demands. In fact, when we were looking for property to build our office in Colorado, one of my requirements was that it had to be near a biking and walking path.

For me, being physically fit and healthy is a huge part of coping with the demands of leadership. When I am overweight, eating poorly, and sedentary, I find that I get very sluggish. My body is sluggish, and my mind is sluggish. And you know what else? My heart and spirit get sluggish too. This is something that one of my mentors taught me many years ago. Jody Dillow and I began the "run for lunch bunch" in the Vienna woods near our office back in the 1980s. It led up to running that 1986 marathon I mentioned in the preface. Several of us got into the habit of running every day at noon.

Moses began his career as a workaholic, which is clear from reading Exodus 18. After we read the story about his encounter with his father-in-law, we quickly learn that Moses sent away his wife and children to live with her parents because he had too much work. How many times have leaders made the same mistake, shortchanging their families because the demands of work are too great? How many spouses and children grow bitter against God because His work keeps the family in waiting? How many kids wait at home for their mommy or daddy and struggle with one disappointed promise after another? For Moses, it's pretty clear from the beginning of chapter 18 that he had a problem:

> Now Jethro, the priest of Midian and father-in-law of Moses, heard of everything God had done for Moses and for his people Israel, and how the LORD had brought Israel out of Egypt.
>
> *After Moses had sent away his wife Zipporah, his father-in-law Jethro received her and her two sons.* One son was named Gershom, for Moses said, "I have become an alien in a foreign land"; and the other was named Eliezer, for he said, "My father's God was my helper; he saved me from the sword of Pharaoh."
>
> Jethro, Moses' father-in-law, together with Moses' sons and wife, came to him in the desert, where he was camped near the mountain of God. Jethro had sent word to him, *"I, your father-in-law Jethro, am coming to you with your wife and her two sons."* (Ex. 18:1–6)

HOW MANY TIMES HAVE LEADERS MADE THE SAME MISTAKE, SHORTCHANGING THEIR FAMILIES BECAUSE THE DEMANDS OF WORK ARE TOO GREAT?

A lot of us face the same challenge as Moses. We often take on big leadership responsibilities in the same years that we also have a young family at home. The early days of my leadership career happened to coincide with the early years of being a parent. The year I became president of our ministry, our older children were ages eleven and nine, and our twins were five. I've always had passion to be a great father and to be available for my children. I told the board when I took the job, "I will not sacrifice my kids for this position." The great thing is that they agreed with me and supported me in this commitment in the years that followed. When I got home from work, it was family time. When I got home from trips, I would spend extra time with my family to make up for my absence. I called these "TRDs"—travel recovery days. I did not go straight back to the office, but rather straight home to the family.

> AS WE GET OLDER AND LOOK BACK ON OUR LIVES, WHO SAYS THAT THEY WISH THEY HAD SPENT MORE TIME AT THE OFFICE?

Donna and my children are a high priority to me and always have been. In the days when we were raising our kids, she and I would hire babysitters so we could have our own dates. We regularly practiced getting away overnight to spend some time together, *alone,* because we both believe that dating is more important after marriage than before marriage. We wanted to make sure that when the kids grew up and left, we would still be in love with each other. And we are still in love today as empty nesters. We are also thankful that our four adult children and their spouses turned out so great and have a close relationship with us to this day.

I remember one year when Jeremy was twelve, it was apparent to us that he needed some special attention from Daddy. He was our middle child—between his older brother, Mark, and the twins. I was in the pressure cooker at work, but I decided he really needed some daddy time to himself. So I took three days off work to take him mountain biking on Mackinac Island in Michigan, as he was in a biking phase. The trip was a great time of biking, pizza, and undivided time with my son. We rode and talked and laughed and played. Having four children, I quickly learned that they each need one-on-one time through the year, not just family time when we are all together. Individual time with each child is critical because all kids—yes, yours, too—tend to fight with each other when they are all clumped together.

Fast-forward to the present. Jeremy is now married with his first son. He told me the other day that he still looks back on that trip as the pinnacle of his childhood memories with me—and it is a model for him for how he wants to be a father to his children. I remember how hard it was to take those days away from my office—but looking back on it today, what could be more important? As we get older and look back on our lives, who says that they wish they had spent more time at the office?

The other challenge I faced with a houseful of kids was *when* to have the time to take care of my body. I'm not a morning person, and trying to get some exercise when I came home from work was impossible. Donna needed relief from the children when I got home from the office. So I started to do my workouts at lunchtime. For me this was a great life pattern, and it's continued for thirty years.

I don't know what will work for you, but find a way to care for your temple—the only body you will ever have. For me, working out during the workday has been the best answer. If I don't have a lunch appointment, I'm going to be on my bicycle, working out, or walking during my lunch hour. Walking or running is great when I travel because I can do it virtually anywhere. I take advantage of hotel gyms that are getting better all the time.

Don't feel guilty about taking an hour or longer. You probably work way more than forty hours a week anyway. If you are in church ministry, you probably work in the evenings quite a lot. I often work late, and I travel about a third of my time. Don't feel guilty for taking a chunk of time in the middle of the day for yourself. The better you take care of yourself, the better you're going to be for your people and for your family. I believe it makes me a much more effective leader and a better husband and father.

JETHRO—THE BIBLE'S FIRST MANAGEMENT CONSULTANT

In Exodus 18 we read about the first management consultant in the Bible, and his name was Jethro. I don't think he got paid for his hours—he was, after all, the father-in-law. I'm a big believer in *good* management consultants. Through the years, we've wasted a lot of money on consultants who did no more than tell us what time it was using our own watch. In my preface I mentioned *The Management Myth* by Matthew Stewart, a career management consultant who wrote, "How can so many who know so little make so much [money] by telling other people how to do the jobs they are paid to know how to do?"[1]

Moses had good intentions. After all, look at all the pressure that God placed upon him. I'm sure he wondered, *How can I take care of all these people, their food, water, and all the Ten Commandments and the tabernacle stuff, and still make time to play with my own kids?* I'm sure if *Zipporah* complained, as many workaholics' wives will do, he had plenty of spiritual justification for his neglect. It seems to me that Moses was the classic workaholic, even though he was doing it all for God! After all, God was the one who laid the responsibility on him in the first place. For some reason, Moses hadn't quite figured out how to delegate. Perhaps because he was the classic control freak with the purest of intentions—trying to please God and be faithful.

> MOSES WAS THE CLASSIC CONTROL FREAK WITH THE PUREST OF INTENTIONS— TRYING TO PLEASE GOD AND BE FAITHFUL.

The good news is that God sent Moses a messenger—the management consultant Jethro—and Moses had the heart to listen to him. Never waste money on consultants if you're not going to take their advice. My friend Tom Beck tells me that the most frustrating part of being a consultant is just that: Many times, people don't have the courage to take his advice. All a consultant can do is listen and advise. Fortunately Moses listened to his father-in-law and took action to change.

I love reading how this consultation played out. When Jethro arrived back in the camp with his daughter and two grandsons,

Moses bragged to his father-in-law about all the amazing things that had happened. The Bible does not say if Moses took time to play with his kids or get reconnected with his wife. We have to leave that part to our imaginations. I love how humble Jethro was as he patiently listened to his son-in-law—good consultants begin with a lot of listening:

> So Moses went out to meet his father-in-law and bowed down and kissed him. They greeted each other and then went into the tent. Moses told his father-in-law about everything the LORD had done to Pharaoh and the Egyptians for Israel's sake and about all the hardships they had met along the way and how the LORD had saved them.
>
> Jethro was delighted to hear about all the good things the LORD had done for Israel in rescuing them from the hand of the Egyptians. (Ex. 18:7–9)

That night as Jethro rested he must have pondered what he should say to his son-in-law. I have a wonderful father-in-law, Mark Bubeck, a godly man who has given me such great advice over the years. My own father has been gone for twenty-five years, so Mark has been my only dad during most of my adult years of leadership. I so appreciate how often he affirms me. I couldn't ask for a greater father-in-law, whom I have called "Dad," over the years. He encourages me not only in my work but also in how I have taken care of his daughter and his grandchildren. And as my children are getting married and having their own children, I appreciate his concerns in a whole new light. Now my kids are providing him great-grandchildren—it doesn't get any better than that!

Jethro loved and respected Moses in the same way. It was not until the next day that Jethro truly got the picture of why Moses was so busy. It says in verses 13 and 14 that Jethro watched and observed, like any good consultant would. And then it was time for Moses to hear the consultant's input as Jethro got real about the big mistake he saw Moses making:

> When his father-in-law saw all that Moses was doing for the people, he said, "What is this you are doing for the people? Why do you alone sit as judge, while all these people stand around you from morning till evening?" … Moses' father-in-law replied, "What you are doing is not good." (Ex. 18:14, 17)

SPREAD THE LOAD

Jethro then taught his son-in-law about delegation and mentoring. I love it when consultants actually have solutions to the problems they observe. Jethro had the solution: Spread the load! If Moses kept working the way he had been working, he would've eventually crashed and burned; Jethro told him, "You cannot handle it alone!"

Problem: "Moses' father-in-law replied, 'What you are doing is not good. You and these people who come to you will only wear yourselves out. *The work is too heavy for you; you cannot handle it alone'"* (Ex. 18:17–18).

Solution: "Listen now to me and I will give you some advice, and may God be with you. You must be the people's representative before God and bring their disputes to him. Teach them the decrees and laws, and show them the way to live and the duties they are to perform. But select capable men from all the people—men who fear God, trustworthy men who hate dishonest gain—and appoint them as officials over thousands, hundreds, fifties and tens. Have them serve as judges for the people at all times, but have them bring every difficult case to you; the simple cases they can decide themselves. That will make your load lighter, because they will share it with you. If you do this and God so commands, *you will be able to stand the strain, and all these people will go home satisfied"* (Ex. 18:19–23).

Did you get that? It was a win-win—Moses could take a breather and focus on his tasks, and the people would actually be happier. In addition, Moses got his wife and children back. Jethro brought such clear insight to the problem that plagues so many leaders: the plague of false indispensability. *Only I can do the job,* some leaders think. But honestly, no one likes working under control freaks. The boss gets overworked, and the workers aren't happy. I have seen in our ministry that the more decisions we can push downstream, the more empowered people feel and the more satisfied they become in their work.

Ronald Reagan was one of our great presidents in modern times, and I loved his leadership because he came to Berlin and had the courage to ignore his handlers and speak boldly to Mikhail

Gorbachev: "Mr. Gorbachev, tear down this wall!" It worked, and the world changed on November 9, 1989, as the wall came down. As I said in my introduction, I was there that day and witnessed history's greatest prison break. That act of leadership changed the world for good. Many criticized him for lack of attention to the details. Some said he was asleep at the wheel. He was not an early riser and did not work late into the evening. But I don't think his critics understood good leadership. He proved to be an extremely capable leader, and his strengths were communication, vision casting, and staying focused on the primary goals. Reagan worked hard each day, headed to the gym at the end of the afternoon, and then had Nancy time and personal time in the evenings.

> THERE IS NO LIMIT TO WHAT A MAN CAN DO OR WHERE HE CAN GO IF HE DOESN'T MIND WHO GETS THE CREDIT.
> —FROM A SIGN ON THE DESK OF PRESIDENT RONALD REAGAN IN THE WHITE HOUSE

He was not a workaholic. Reagan had a sign on his desk that said, "There is no limit to what a man can do or where he can go if he doesn't mind who gets the credit."[2] Those are the words of a delegator.

So how do we afford the time to get away and take care of our own bodies and souls? Where do we make room in our schedules for our marriages and families? I think a lot of it has to do with good delegation. If I surround myself with a good team and allow those people to lead, then I don't have to be a control freak. I follow the philosophy that says: "My job is to lead the organization, not control it." To me, leadership is about setting direction, casting vision, and coaching my team. Management is about control, and control is not leadership. If you have to control every decision, then you definitely won't have any time for yourself or your family. And forget about leaving for a really great vacation. But if you're an effective leader and delegator, you will have plenty of time for a balanced life. Sure, I get pulled into the difficult decisions, but I am not trying to control everything.

Howard Hendricks was one of my early mentors in seminary in Dallas, Texas. He taught us young men the importance of loving our wives and always giving them our time and attention. He often said, "The best thing you can ever do for your children is to love their mother." He also taught us how to divide work life from home life.

I still remember him telling the story of his drive home from work every evening. As he drove home from the seminary, he crossed a certain bridge that lead into his neighborhood. He told us he would toss all of his concerns and worries over that bridge so that they did not distract him when he got home. Then he said with a big smile, "And you know, when I crossed that bridge the next morning, they were there waiting for me!" I determined during those years I would do the same thing. I decided that even though I was in seminary and had tons of homework every evening, I would always go to bed at the same time Donna did so we could be together. I worked hard during the day so I did not have to work late. It's a practice I have followed for thirty-five years now, at least when we are both in the same time zone and accommodations! Nothing is so important at work that it should rob me of my family or my marriage.

It was Jethro who taught Moses about avoiding the pitfalls of micromanagement. Moses was a control freak who, fortunately for him and his family, learned the lesson and changed. Leaders must learn to spread the load to a team of leaders surrounding them.

VACATIONS — DO YOU REALLY?

I am part of a network of nonprofit CEOs who give such great encouragement to Donna and me. These CEOs and I walk in the same shoes and have the unusual ability to really help one another with our problems. Every February, twenty couples get together for our annual retreat. It is one of the highlights of our year and one of the first events I lock into my calendar annually. I see among my colleagues one problem that crops up year after year—the lack of vacations. Many of us have a hard time taking real vacations. It's part of that "I'm indispensable" syndrome. Certainly control freaks can't take good vacations because things might get out of control while they're gone! I am not accusing my CEO buddies of being control freaks, but I can see how busy they all are and how they feel guilty walking away from the demands of their jobs to "selfishly" tend to their own souls. Even ministry leaders struggle with this, and sometimes more than other leaders because of intense spiritual conscientiousness. After all, meeting great spiritual needs is never done. Many seasoned leaders struggle with this tension more every year as demands on their leadership increase.

Do you actually take the vacation time that is given to you? And do you take *real* vacations—with your loved ones and away from work? I see a lot of people in ministry and in the marketplace combine vacations with work commitments. They are like "almost vacations, *but not quite*." I get the rationale—the company can pay for the plane tickets, and I can add a little vacation to the trip. But it seems to me that there's not a lot of pure vacation going on. When I go on a one- or two-week vacation with Donna or my family, I find that it takes me one or two days just to decompress.

The two excuses I hear the most for not taking vacation are *finances* and *time:* "I just don't have the money for a real vacation." And of course the one I hear the most, "I just can't seem to find the time." For both of these problems, planning would solve them. It really comes down to a choice of priorities. We all have the choice each year of how we will fill our next 365 days, and we do manage to always fit in that which we say is nonnegotiable. If you say that your marriage, family, and personal sanity really are important to you, then you would plan the anchors of vacation into your yearly calendar. We view a yearly calendar like filling an aquarium with rocks, stones, and pebbles. Donna and I put the big rocks of vacation on our schedule before our life fills up with all the stones and pebbles of the tyranny of the urgent. If we don't plan our time, others will plan it for us. We cherish those uninterrupted family vacations and also empty-nest times away. Because we practiced this over the years, we still have a close relationship with each other even after our kids left home.

To handle the money piece, Donna and I started a vacation savings account a number of years ago with an online bank. With every paycheck, we drop a specified amount automatically into that fully isolated vacation savings account. When it comes time for vacation, we have the debit card associated with that account that we use for the entire vacation, and we don't feel guilty spending "now money" on our holiday.

And of course, once you go on vacation, can you turn off your work? With everything coming to our smartphones today, this challenge is harder than ever. That is a tough one that I have learned the hard way. I once had a family vacation totally ruined when I checked my voice mail. That was the moment I realized that it was foolish to mix vacation and work. I heard the voicemail about some negative event that happened back at the office. I honestly don't remember what it was to this day. But a cloud slipped over my mind for the rest of our camping trip up in Michigan. When I got home, I realized that there was nothing I could have done about the problem anyway while I was gone.

Ever since then, I try faithfully to go on a self-imposed electronic vacation. Now it's even harder with email, voice mail, text messaging, Facebook, Twitter, and the Web. This past summer my oldest son, Mark, and I held each other accountable on our family vacation to stay away from work-related electronic communications. That's why Donna and I love going to Mexico on our vacations. We're not that far away from home, but we're in another country, and it makes it easier for me to shut off the electronics. I lock my laptop and cell phone in the room safe and check for emergency phone messages once a day. I trained my assistant to know what constitutes a real emergency.

When our children were little, the best investment we ever made for the family was in a motor home. We had so many great vacations driving across the country in our own little family sanctuary. To this day, our grown children talk about how much they loved those motor home vacations on which we visited national parks and saw a lot of the western United States. I know another reason they loved it so much was because they had 100 percent of their mommy and daddy.

I want to camp on this issue of vacation a little more—excuse the pun! We all need our vacations, but so many people don't even take the time they have coming to them. I have people in my own organization I have to hound on this point year after year. I make my direct reports tell me about their vacations each year, and I hold them accountable to take the time that is given to them. It makes them better people, and I believe it is something we should never feel guilty about. When it is time for your vacation, just stop working. Let things go. Remember that your family needs you just as much as those at work do.

I am not sure why this is not hard for me, but I think it has something to do with struggles I have observed in leaders who have failed. "What will it profit a man if he gains the whole world, and loses his own soul?" Jesus asked (Mark 8:36 NKJV). I would agree and add, "What will it profit a man if he gains the praise and admiration of his colleagues and loses his own marriage and/ or children?"

Some of this has to do with culture. I'm pure German, and we Germans generally work hard and play hard. We have no trouble taking every single vacation day coming to us. I don't know why that seems to be so difficult for many Americans. Of course I'm an American, too, but I was raised in a very German home, as I've already shared. Somehow that heritage had a big impact on my adulthood. My mom and dad loved their vacations. We went to Daytona Beach, Florida, every summer to hang out on the beach for two weeks. I watched my parents sit, soak, and read as they recharged their batteries.

Research shows that Americans are the worst vacation takers on planet Earth. Almost fifty million Americans are vacation deprived, according to Expedia.com.[3] The facts show that 34 percent of employed US adults report they don't use all their vacation days each year.[4] Here's an interesting report I discovered about the best and the worst nationalities when it comes to taking vacations:

> The Best: France wins the distinction for receiving and taking the most vacation days out of those countries surveyed. Employed adults in France receive an average of 38 days of vacation each year, compared to 13 days for U.S. employed adults and 26 days for employed adults in Great Britain. And French workers take an average of 36 vacation days per year, compared to 8 days for employed adults in Japan, 11 days for U.S. employed adults, 23 for employed adults in Austria and 24 days for employed adults in Great Britain. [Germans get 27 days on average.]

> The Worst: *Throughout the eight years that the Vacation Deprivation survey has been conducted, the U.S. has long held the dismaying distinction of being the*

country with the worst vacationing habits. Employed
adults in the United States receive the least vacation
days per year (13 days).[5]

Spread the Load—Build a Team

Okay, the advice from Jethro was clear—build a team, and learn to
delegate: "That will make your load lighter, because they will share it
with you" (Ex. 18:22). I think this is great advice for the many high-
capacity, high-octane, type A personality leaders we find in business
and nonprofit leadership today. It's so easy to get out of balance in
our personal lives, and, unfortunately, the damage from this mistake
doesn't show up until it's usually too late. I have seen too many leaders fail in their professional lives for personal reasons that have to do
with this kind of lack of balance—like Moses, we need to learn to
get a life.

Jethro helped Moses learn to be team centered in his leadership.
And over time he learned to develop others who took a significant
role on his team. Coach Bear Bryant at the University of Alabama
was famous for allowing his assistants to make a lot of key calls in
football games. He believed that if you don't let the assistant coaches
coach, you won't ever get any good assistants.

Moses figured out why teams are so important to success. I will
finish this chapter with four powerful benefits that result when you
build a good, solid leadership team. These are the things that Moses
experienced by working through his teams.

If You Work through a Team, You Are More Likely to Succeed

When the Amalekites attacked the Israelites, a great team effort brought about the victory. Moses sent Joshua to lead the battle, because Joshua was his number two man. Then Aaron and Hur went to the top of the hill with Moses:

> As long as Moses held up his hands, the Israelites were winning, but whenever he lowered his hands, the Amalekites were winning. When Moses' hands grew tired, they took a stone and put it under him and he sat on it. Aaron and Hur held his hands up— one on one side, one on the other—so that his hands remained steady till sunset. So Joshua overcame the Amalekite army with the sword. (Ex. 17:11–13)

There are several great leadership lessons here. Moses has enough wisdom to send a young man to do the tough job of leading the battle. He and the older guys went to perform the backup prayer. Moses let Joshua lead the battle even though Moses was still clearly in charge. That's an example of great leadership mentoring. We can also see here again the future potential of Joshua. Notice that in verse 14 the Lord says to Moses, "Write this on a scroll as something to be remembered and *make sure that Joshua hears it,* because I will completely blot out

GOD HIMSELF POSITIONED JOSHUA TO TAKE OVER FROM MOSES IN THE FUTURE. AND MOSES WAS OKAY WITH THAT.

the memory of Amalek from under heaven." God Himself positioned Joshua to take over from Moses in the future. And Moses was okay with that.

IF YOU WORK THROUGH A TEAM, YOU ARE LESS LIKELY TO BURN OUT

The lesson is clear from what Moses learned from his father-in-law:

> Moses' father-in-law replied, "What you are doing is not good. You and these people who come to you will *only wear yourselves out. The work is too heavy for you; you cannot handle it alone....* If you do this and God so commands, *you will be able to stand the strain, and all these people will go home satisfied.*" (Ex. 18:17–18, 23)

How many leaders throw in the towel because they can't stand the strain any longer? I tell you now, learn how to delegate responsibility and share the load with your team. If you don't have a team, that's your first job: *Find one.* Maybe you think you can't afford it? Then look for volunteers or even interns. We cannot go at it alone when it comes to the heavy demands of leadership.

IF YOU WORK THROUGH A TEAM, YOU DO BETTER WORK

God instructed Moses to share the load with the seventy elders. It wasn't just sharing the load—this required sharing the spiritual responsibility and authority. God took some of the Spirit that was with Moses and put it on the elders. I love that picture of shared leadership gifting and responsibility. Even if Moses went on vacation, the good work would continue:

> The LORD said to Moses: "Bring me seventy of Israel's elders who are known to you as leaders and officials among the people. Have them come to the Tent of Meeting, that they may stand there with you. I will come down and speak with you there, *and I will take of the Spirit that is on you and put the Spirit on them.* They will help you carry the burden of the people so that you will not have to carry it alone." (Num. 11:16–17)

IF YOU WORK THROUGH A TEAM, YOU ENSURE LONG-TERM CONTINUITY OF YOUR WORK

If everyone relies just on me, then once I'm gone, everything will collapse. But if I share the load with a team, even if team members come and go, there is continuity over time. The best way to ensure that my contribution will last is to be part of a team that shares the leadership responsibility. I'm so thankful for the young leaders on my current team, all of whom believe in the vision and will make sure we get to the promised land (achieve our goals) when I'm no longer around.

> THE BEST WAY TO ENSURE THAT MY CONTRIBUTION WILL LAST IS TO BE PART OF A TEAM THAT SHARES THE LEADERSHIP RESPONSIBILITY.

I know they'll do things differently, which is fine with me—I'm asking them to do things differently now! I see this as assurance that we don't end up turning our work over to fools like that despondent writer of Ecclesiastes:

> So I hated life, because the work that is done under the sun was grievous to me. All of it is meaningless, a chasing after the wind. I hated all the things I had toiled for under the sun, because I must leave them to the one who comes after me. *And who knows whether he will be a wise man or a fool?* Yet he will have control over all the work into which I have poured my effort and skill under the sun. This too is meaningless. (Eccl. 2:17–19)

Those are pretty depressing words, right? The best way I can see to avoid that kind of end to my leadership contribution is to build a strong team and share the leadership load with them.

6

LEADERSHIP COMMANDMENT #6: THOU SHALT SWEAT THE SMALL STUFF

When Moses finished reciting all these words to all Israel, he said
to them, "Take to heart all the words I have solemnly declared
to you this day, so that you may command your children to obey
carefully all the words of this law. They are not just idle words for
you—they are your life. By them you will live long in the land
you are crossing the Jordan to possess." (Deut. 32:45–47)

Big Idea: Character always trumps gifting in leadership. And character
is made up of many small acts of integrity. Effective leaders have to
pay attention to the small stuff even if they are big-picture thinkers.

I turned in four months of expense reports this week. It took me a
whole afternoon of sifting through receipts and online statements to

get it all together. I honestly hate doing my expense reconciliations, though if you are an accountant or a CPA, I bet you love it. I guess some of us big thinkers get annoyed by these kinds of tiny details. But I do pay attention. Recently, our finance clerk said to me, "Hans, you do the best job of anyone in documenting your expenses." I thought to myself, then replied, "I have to. I have to set an example, and I am held to a higher standard."

This is hard for me. Ask anyone who knows me, and he or she will tell you, "Hans is a big-idea guy. Give him the forty-thousand-foot view. Put it on one page if you want him to read it. Details bore him." I am guilty of all those accusations. But as I said, I do care and force myself to pay attention to the small stuff.

Moses was a man of great integrity. He sweated the small stuff. Here is how the dictionary defines integrity: (1) "adherence to moral and ethical principles; soundness of moral character; honesty"; (2) "the state of being whole, entire, or undiminished: to preserve the integrity of the empire"; (3) "a sound, unimpaired, or perfect condition: the integrity of a ship's hull."[1]

Recently, we watched Tiger Woods devolve into an average professional golfer after a career of reigning supreme at the top of his game. What happened? He did not sweat the small stuff *off* the golf course. There are many examples of small stuff that if ignored will take you out. I hesitate to even list them here, as there are so many facets to being a person of integrity. The list I've compiled highlights some of the obvious ones that have destroyed many a person. Just last month we had to let someone go in our finance office because he secretly "borrowed" less than two hundred dollars from petty cash. This person had crossed the line several other times in the past when it came to issues

of integrity in the workplace. I was sad to see his departure because of
the lack of integrity—*I really liked the guy*. Examples of integrity battles
I've witnessed in my career include the following:

> Truth in finances
> Abuse of finances
> Relationship with members of the opposite sex
> Marital faithfulness
> Ethical issues
> Truthfulness
> Fulfilling promises
> Personal use of time in the workplace
> Personal use of corporate property
> Life on the road—lots of small stuff looming to
> take you down
> Navigating the world of the Internet and media

While I was writing this book, I wrote to a number of people
and asked them for their definition of finishing well. I asked, "How
would you describe a successful life when you are looking back from
the finish line?" I really like the answer that author and speaker John
Maxwell emailed me:

> I have always stated that my definition of success
> is that those closest to me love and respect me the
> most. So I will have finished well if at the end …
> those closest to me, who knew me inside and out,
> love and respect me the most.[2]

Those who are closest to us know us inside and out. If they believe we have integrity, then I would say we are doing a good job sweating the small stuff. It's sad to see leaders both in the marketplace and in ministry who get a lot of public adoration but have lost the respect of their families and friends.

> IN LOOKING FOR PEOPLE TO HIRE, YOU LOOK FOR THREE QUALITIES: INTEGRITY, INTELLIGENCE, AND ENERGY. AND IF THEY DON'T HAVE THE FIRST, THE OTHER TWO WILL KILL YOU.
> —WARREN BUFFETT, CEO OF BERKSHIRE HATHAWAY

As I am writing this chapter, Mark Hurd just lost his job as the star turnaround CEO at HP in Silicon Valley, California. By the time you read this, he will be long forgotten and out of the headlines. HP ousted Mark Hurd for submitting inaccurate expense reports connected to a contractor who did marketing for the company. While investigating the contract worker's claim that Hurd sexually harassed her, HP said it discovered Hurd falsified expenses connected to her. The company reported that in "numerous instances … the contractor received compensation … where there was not a legitimate business purpose," according to HP general counsel.[3]

Five years of brilliant leadership came to an end because of an indiscretion in his expense account. It had to do with an attractive woman and some questionable expenses, but there was no illicit sexual behavior. Hurd claimed that someone else had messed up his expense reports. Someone was not sweating the small stuff!

What disheartens me is the way the rest of the story played out. Hurd then received a twenty-eight-million-dollar golden parachute. Great reward for messing up, huh? What would happen to most of us if we were caught in this kind of scandal? We would be shown the door immediately. Oh well, God is keeping the real score!

Not about Control or Legalism

Recently, I spoke on this idea of sweating the small stuff as a leader. Someone in the audience asked me a great question: "How do you keep from being a control freak but still sweat the small stuff?" Great question! This chapter is about integrity, not control. It is about keeping a close eye on the little attacks waged on our lives and hearts every day as a leader. We have to pay attention to the hairline cracks that can become a chasm, taking us out of our leadership position entirely.

Sweating the Small Stuff Is Not about Legalism

Unfortunately a lot of people mistake legalism for spirituality. Jesus had a big problem with the people who did this in His day— they were called the Pharisees. They were religious control freaks. They love to make silly rules for us to follow. I don't think God ever had that in mind. We have freedom in Christ, and we are a community that should deal with one another from a position of grace.

Sweating the Small Stuff Is Not about Control

I said enough in the last chapter about control freaks, so I don't need to say much more. We do have to pay attention to issues of integrity both in ourselves and in the people on our team; however, that is not a license for micromanagement.

Sweating the Small Stuff Means Paying Attention to Character

God pays very close attention to our hearts. Jesus said in the Sermon on the Mount, "Blessed are the pure in heart, for they will see God" (Matt. 5:8).

God Is Watching Us

The line "God is watching you" is from a popular song from long ago. The lyrics are true. Moses knew that and referred to it in his moving "Prayer of Moses" found in Psalm 90: "You have set our iniquities before you, our secret sins in the light of your presence" (v. 8). We can fool some of the people all of the time, but we can fool God none of the time. Moses knew this truth and lived out a life of integrity.

One place where that integrity showed up time and again was in his faithfulness to God's commands. Here is a statement that occurs over and over again in the Old Testament: "Moses did as the Lord commanded him" (Num. 27:22). This phrase appears ninety-four times in the Old Testament! It is true that the devil is in the details, and it's usually in small acts of disobedience that leaders stumble. Not in the big slashes but in the dozens of tiny cuts. Moses was not only a man of vision, but also a man of detail. Much of the content of the books of Moses in the Old Testament is about the minute details of legislation in lifestyle and obedience in building the tabernacle that God told him to build. He knew how important it was to play by God's rules. That's why at the very end of his life when he passed the baton to Joshua, he reminded everyone again of what it takes to be successful in God's economy:

> When Moses finished reciting all these words to all Israel, he said to them, "Take to heart *all the words* I have solemnly declared to you this day, so that you may command your children to *obey carefully all the words of this law.* They are not just idle words for you—they are your life. By them you will live long in the land you are crossing the Jordan to possess." (Deut. 32:45–47)

God Uses People with Fatal Flaws

Here's a quick quiz: What was Moses' fatal flaw? What was his greatest character weakness? If you answered *anger,* you're absolutely right. Time and again when the people grumbled against Moses, as we rehearsed in chapter 4, his anger flared.

We see an example of this in Exodus 16: "However, some of them paid no attention to Moses; they kept part of it until morning, but it was full of maggots and began to smell. *So Moses was angry with them*" (Ex. 16:20).

I found it curious that we never once read that Moses asked for forgiveness from his people for that anger problem. I wonder if he did. Maybe that was another of his flaws. I know he asked God's forgiveness. I think it's important, when we fail in front of our people, to admit we're wrong and ask for their forgiveness.

> THE MOST IMPORTANT PERSUASION TOOL YOU HAVE IN YOUR ENTIRE ARSENAL IS INTEGRITY.
> —ZIG ZIGLAR

I don't have a big problem with anger in the workplace. I've exploded in anger more on the home front against inanimate objects. One day, Donna came running to the front door, thinking I was being attacked outside our house. Instead, I was standing out on the front porch all by myself in a fit of anger. On this particular November evening I got so angry at the Christmas lights I was trying to string out front that I smashed three different strings of tiny lights to pieces right there on the front porch. Apparently Donna heard me yelling and opened the front door, wondering what in the world was going on. You see, every Christmas, I get upset at what I call the Christmas-light conspiracy. Every January I put the lights away in their proper boxes, and they all work perfectly. Then something magical happens during the year. All I know is that I pull out the strings in November, turn them on—and some of them don't work! I don't know about you, but I do not have the patience to go down an entire string of Christmas lights, one by one, looking for the culprit.

That particular Christmas, Donna opened the front door and found me dancing on the lights and laughed her head off. I jumped up and down and smashed three strings of lights to smithereens—*and it felt so good!* She said she had never seen me angrier. I'm just glad that I got angry at Christmas lights and not a person.

Anger is a powerful emotion. I know that my anger compared to that of Moses is more than trivial. But anger is anger, and it often brings out the worst in us. The anger problem did get Moses and Aaron into big trouble. It was ultimately that emotion that kept them from entering the Promised Land.

Numbers 20 is a longer passage but important for me to include in its entirety here. The story is usually called "water from the rock." You might remember a previous and very similar instance recorded in Exodus 17. In that situation, the people grumbled and quarreled with Moses as they were camped at Rephidim. So much so that Moses thought that they were going to stone him, but he managed to keep a cool head. God instructed him to take some elders with him and go to the rock at Horeb: "Strike the rock, and the water will come out of it for the people to drink" (v. 6). Moses did what he was told, and the water flowed for the people. But in this second case in Numbers 20, twenty years later, God specifically told Moses to *speak* to the rock—*not to strike it with his staff.* I don't know why God changed His strategy this time around. We are not told. Maybe it was some kind of test of obedience for Moses. Here is how the story unfolds:

> INSTEAD OF SPEAKING GENTLY TO THE ROCK AS GOD COMMANDED, MOSES POUNDED THE ROCK TWICE WITH HIS STAFF. THIS OUTBURST EMBARRASSED GOD AND HUMILIATED THE PEOPLE.

PROBLEM: NO WATER FOR THE PEOPLE

In the first month the whole Israelite community arrived at the Desert of Zin, and they stayed at Kadesh. There Miriam died and was buried.

Now there was no water for the community, and the people gathered in opposition to Moses and Aaron. They quarreled with Moses and said, "If only we had died when our brothers fell dead before the LORD! Why did you bring the LORD's community into this desert, that we and our livestock should die here? Why did you bring us up out of Egypt to this terrible place? It has no grain or figs, grapevines or pomegranates. And there is no water to drink!" (Num. 20:1–5)

SOLUTION: SPEAK TO THE ROCK

Moses and Aaron went from the assembly to the entrance to the Tent of Meeting and fell facedown, and the glory of the LORD appeared to them. The LORD said to Moses, "Take the staff, and you and your brother Aaron gather the assembly together. *Speak to that rock before their eyes and it will pour out its water.* You will bring water out of the rock for the community so they and their livestock can drink." (vv. 6–8)

Response: Moses Strikes the Rock Twice

> So Moses took the staff from the LORD's presence, just as he commanded him. He and Aaron gathered the assembly together in front of the rock and Moses said to them, "Listen, you rebels, must we bring you water out of this rock?" *Then Moses raised his arm and struck the rock twice with his staff.* Water gushed out, and the community and their livestock drank. (vv. 9–11)

Result: Moses and Aaron Are Punished

> But the LORD said to Moses and Aaron, "*Because you did not trust in me enough to honor me as holy in the sight of the Israelites, you will not bring this community into the land I give them.*" (v. 12)

Apparently this was the worst display of anger exhibited by Moses in front of God and the Israelites. Instead of speaking gently to the rock as God commanded, Moses pounded the rock twice with his staff. This outburst embarrassed God and humiliated the people.

Notice that the punishment applied to Aaron as well. It shows me how my own leadership mistakes can impact the other leaders on my team. We pay the penalty for one another's mistakes if we have a good, tight leadership team. The good news was that Moses and Aaron had a leadership team that worked well together, but the bad news was that the failure of the top leader affected the others. The punishment that God gave to Moses and Aaron was clear: They would not enter the Promised Land. Why did this sin of anger warrant such an extreme penalty? Nowhere in the Old Testament is the Bible clear on exactly why. However, tucked away in chapter 1 of Deuteronomy is another reference to Moses' anger problem, which was the cause of God's discipline on his life: "Because of you the LORD became angry with me also and said, '*You shall not enter it, either*'" (Deut. 1:37).

A LEADER'S BALANCE BAR

Integrity is important in God's economy, and it should be critical in our leadership as well. What disqualifies people from being on our leadership team? What makes you invite them to get off the bus? I've always viewed people's contribution to the team like the two ends of a balance bar. On one side of the balance bar is the weight of *tasks,* or "professional skills." On the other side of the balance bar is the weight of *personal relationships*—what I call "people skills." We have asked some people to leave our organization because the conflict and destruction caused on the personal-relationship side greatly outweighed their professional contribution. At other times, someone's people skills rocked—*everyone loved the person*—but his or her professional skills were a disaster. It doesn't matter how good your people skills are if you can't deliver the task required by the job. And, on the other side, it doesn't matter how well you perform the tasks of the job if you can't get along with others on the team.

THE LEADER'S BALANCE BAR

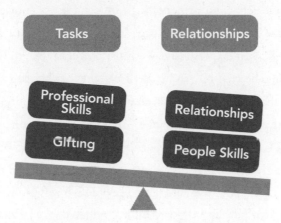

Sweating the small stuff to me is about living a life of integrity. The ideal leader has balance in his or her life, good competencies, and a solid character on both sides of the balance beam, which reminds me of another great Old Testament character, David. The Bible describes him as a "man after [God's] own heart" (1 Sam. 13:14). I always liked the balance of the following description of David found in the book of Psalms, because it shows that being an effective leader takes both integrity of heart (character) *and* skill in leadership: "And David shepherded them with integrity of heart; with skillful hands he led them" (Ps. 78:72).

We recently had to make the painful decision to let go one of the leaders in our ministry because of an overwhelming accumulation of negative weight on his balance bar. It was really hard for me because he's a good personal friend. Bob (not his real name) is such a likable person, with a tremendous amount of vision and skill.

Upon meeting him, you would like him immediately. But Bob lost people's respect because he failed to keep promises, did not follow through, and left commitments unfulfilled. He was not a man of his word and often forgot his word. It reminds me of what Edward Murrow said: "To be persuasive we must be believable; to be believable we must be credible; to be credible we must be truthful."

I find that firing people is often a part of getting an organization back in line with its integrity. Have you ever fired someone and then had people get upset with you because of that decision? Because of confidentiality, we can't really tell people the story behind the story. In cases like the one involving Bob, people who didn't have direct experience working with him wouldn't understand our decision to let him go. But for those who did work with him, there was a great sigh of relief.

After making painful mistakes, I've learned a great deal about how *not* to hire people. My friend Tom the consultant always tells me, "The best time to fire people is before you hire them." One problem is that references are rarely truthful. The other problem is that you cannot know 100 percent of what people are like until they work with you. As a result, these days I spend a lot more time interviewing and checking references than I used to. It's important that we ask former employers not only about the professional-skill side of the equation but also the people side. We ask about how they measure up on their balance bar. And in hiring, I have come to see good attitudes as much more important than a person's professional competence. Someone gave me this great piece of advice once: "Hire for attitude; train for skill." It is something I've certainly put into practice in my office. You can train for skills, but not attitude.

When Jethro the consultant gave Moses advice on appointing elders, he came up with a pretty good list: "But select capable men from all the people—men who fear God, trustworthy men who hate dishonest gain—and appoint them as officials over thousands, hundreds, fifties and tens" (Ex. 18:21).

> HIRE FOR ATTITUDE. TRAIN FOR SKILL.

I look for four things when I interview people to join our team, and it is in these four areas that I also drill their references:

PERSONAL CHARACTER

Does this person possess a good reputation and track record in his or her character? Is he or she known as a person of integrity? Do people speak well of him or her? Is this person personally mature as a mate and family person if married with children? The candidate should display an obvious passion to follow Jesus and a proven track record of spiritual leadership. The person must have a sterling reputation. Not as a workaholic, but as well balanced with a life outside of ministry.

PROFESSIONAL COMPETENCE

Does this person have the skills to get the job done? Is there an experience base of the professional competence necessary to do the job?

PEOPLE CHEMISTRY

Is this person comfortable to be around? Is relating to him or her awkward or easy? This person must be a proven team player and get along well with people. This person will need to get along well on a personal level with the leadership team and his or her direct reports. Personal chemistry can only be determined through an extensive interview process and lots of "face time." I like to take a person to a coffee shop, or take him or her out to lunch, and just hang out with that person to get a feel for who he or she is.

PERCEPTION OF CULTURE

Is this person a good match for our corporate values? Does he or she "get us" as an organization? Is the person passionate about what we are? Has this person's experience in the past given him or her an opportunity to work in an environment similar to ours? A person you hire should display genuine enthusiasm and support of your vision, mission, and values.

MOSES RETIRED A FULFILLED MAN

I used to think it was unfair for God to punish Moses like He did. Two strikes of anger on that rock, and God banished Moses from the Promised Land? But as I've reflected longer on the decision, I've come up with a couple of insights.

First of all, Moses died a fulfilled and satisfied old man. I will visit that story in the final chapter of this book. He was 120 years old when he died, and frankly I think he was tired of being "the man." He was happy to let the young people pick up the mantle of leadership. I love what I do in my leadership responsibility, but I know the day is coming very soon when I will be turning over the wheel to the next person. I will not miss the pressure of these twenty years at the helm. After all, Moses did an amazing amount of heavy lifting for forty years, dragging the Israelites through the desert all the way to the doorstep of the Promised Land. He sweated the small stuff and knew that God was pleased with his leadership.

Second, the forty-year journey of Moses through the desert with the Israelites strikes me as a great model of servant leadership. Remember my definition of a servant leader (chapter 3): when the leader cares more about the good of the organization and its people than his or her own enrichment. It was his role as servant leader that brought them from Egypt to the door of the Promised Land over the course of his forty years at the helm. That was enough for him. Surely Moses was ready to pass the baton and let the next generation lead.

7

LEADERSHIP COMMANDMENT #7: THOU SHALT SPEND TIME IN THE TENT

Then Moses said to him, "If your Presence does not go with us, do not send us up from here. How will anyone know that you are pleased with me and with your people unless you go with us? What else will distinguish me and your people from all the other people on the face of the earth?" And the LORD said to Moses, "I will do the very thing you have asked, because I am pleased with you and I know you by name." (Ex. 33:15–17)

Big Idea: Leaders in ministry cannot succeed in the realms of the spirit without the "God factor." Our relationship with Him affects every aspect of our leadership. Time with Him translates into power for His cause.

This has been the hardest chapter for me to write. Prayer is an area where I feel a great deal of personal failure as a leader. It is so important—I know that, and I see it in the story of Moses—but of all the things I see in Moses that I admire, prayer is the hardest for me to practice. The good news is that I married into a praying family. Donna is the prayer warrior in our family, and she got that from her dad. I really believe that a lot of the blessing on our marriage, family, and ministry has come through the prayers of my godly wife. And her dad—I have never known a person who prays as seriously and aggressively as Mark Bubeck. He's written great books on prayer, including his classic on spiritual warfare, *The Adversary* (Moody).

Moses was also a great man of prayer who walked with God in an unusual way. Just look at what God Himself said about Moses:

> Then the LORD came down in a pillar of cloud; he
> stood at the entrance to the Tent and summoned
> Aaron and Miriam. When both of them stepped
> forward, he said, "Listen to my words:
>
> "When a prophet of the LORD is among you,
>   I reveal myself to him in visions,
>   I speak to him in dreams.
> But this is not true of my servant Moses;
>   he is faithful in all my house.
> *With him I speak face to face,*
>   clearly and not in riddles;
>   *he sees the form of the LORD.*" (Num. 12:5–8)

Wow. Face-to-face. Moses saw the actual form of God! Prayer has never gotten any better than that for any human in history. Recently we had half a day of prayer as part of our regular summer leadership retreat. Twice a year we gather our top leaders together for a leadership retreat to pray about and plan for the future. On this particular occasion we went to a beautiful state park here in Colorado: Castlewood Canyon State Park. One of my staff created a prayer guide, and we sent everyone out on his or her own to spend a couple of hours with God. I found a beautiful rock overlooking a canyon and began to quietly listen to God. At the beginning I said, "Lord, I really don't know what You have for me today. I just know I want to hear from You. I'm not going to bore You with my words. I'm not going to burden You with requests. I just want to listen to You. What do You have for me?" It struck me that day how much listening is a part of prayer.

Because I had been working on this book, I was drawn to the book of Exodus that morning. Providentially God led me to read Exodus 33. I don't know if I have ever read anything that so clearly demonstrates the role of listening in prayer—*not talking*—just receiving without asking:

> Moses said to the LORD, "You have been telling me, 'Lead these people,' but you have not let me know whom you will send with me. You have said, 'I know you by name and you have found favor with me.' If you are pleased with me, *teach me your ways so I may know you* and continue to find favor with you. Remember that this nation is your people." ...

Then Moses said to him, *"If your Presence does not go with us, do not send us up from here.* How will anyone know that you are pleased with me and with your people unless you go with us? What else will distinguish me and your people from all the other people on the face of the earth?"

And the LORD said to Moses, "I will do the very thing you have asked, because I am pleased with you and *I know you by name."* (Ex. 33:12–13, 15–17)

Moses drew a line in the sand that day. He was overwhelmed with his task and sensed a lack of God's power. He wanted his people to stand out as God's people. And he knew that if God was not with him, he was not going anywhere. He said, "Hey, God, remember that these are *Your* people—not mine." Oh, that I would live that way. It is so easy for me to work and to lead on my own strength, in my own little world, with my own gifts and education and position. This is why God loved this guy so much—Moses knew where he was without God! *Nowhere!*

Does anyone see the handprints of God in our ministry or business? Can He be sensed in our midst? Moses knew that the presence of God in their midst was what would distinguish his people from the other people around them. This is such a powerful statement to me about how important it is for me to practice the presence of God. It's such a great reminder to my whole team that He needs to be with us as a group. After our time alone that day in Castlewood Canyon State Park, we came back and sat in a big circle under the park pavilion. I asked everyone to share what God had said to him or her that morning. I was amazed at how much this theme came across to all of us. A fantastic thing happened that morning—we all got the same message! Here is the list of the big theme issues we came up with for that morning as we sat and listened:

> We need to be leaders listening to God.
> We need to be pursuers of God.
> We need to be more about being, less about doing.
> Our relationships with each other are key to God's blessing.

Leadership success comes down to issues of the heart. How can we possibly study the leadership of Moses without observing his relationship with his God? Deuteronomy 34:10 reads, "Since then, no prophet has risen in Israel like Moses, whom the LORD knew face to face." Moses' close relationship with God started at the burning bush, and he kept close to that flame his whole life.

THE TENT OF MEETING

During the years that the Israelites spent in the wilderness under the leadership of Moses, they were not without a "temple" of sorts—it was known as the "tabernacle" or "tent of meeting." Since the Israelites were on the move, no permanent structure could be built, so the tabernacle took the form of an elaborate—and holy—tent structure that could be taken apart and moved. Before the tabernacle was built, it seems that Moses had a more primitive tent that he used to meet with God. This was a "starter tabernacle" of sorts, and Moses spent a lot of time in that tent, listening to God and getting instructions:

Now Moses used to take a tent and pitch it outside the camp some distance away, calling it the "tent of meeting." Anyone inquiring of the LORD would go to the tent of meeting outside the camp. And whenever Moses went out to the tent, all the people rose and stood at the entrances to their tents, watching Moses until he entered the tent. *As Moses went into the tent, the pillar of cloud would come down and stay at the entrance, while the LORD spoke with Moses.* Whenever the people saw the pillar of cloud standing at the entrance to the tent, they all stood and worshiped each at the entrance to his tent. *The LORD would speak to Moses face to face, as a man speaks with his friend.* Then Moses would return to the camp, but his young aide Joshua son of Nun did not leave the tent. (Ex. 33:7–11)

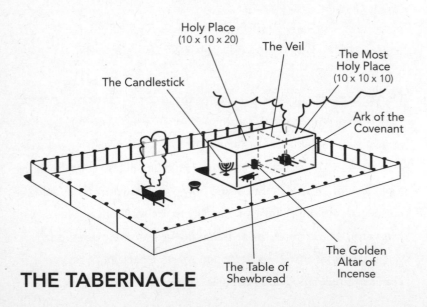

Holy Place
(10 x 10 x 20)

The Veil

The Most Holy Place
(10 x 10 x 10)

The Candlestick

Ark of the Covenant

The Golden Altar of Incense

The Table of Shewbread

THE TABERNACLE

When Moses was in his tent, the people rose and stood at the entrance of their tents to see what was going to happen. Picture a huge camp with many long rows of tents, making up a tent city. At the door of each, the inhabitants of that tent stood poised and anxious for any word. They kept their eyes on their leader as he met with God. Similarly, our people know if we're spending time with God. This is something we cannot fake.

Eventually, they built a more elaborate portable tent of meeting, as described in Exodus 25—31 and 35—40. God spoke to Moses face-to-face in that tent. There's no other place in the Bible where we see this kind of an intimate relationship between a man and God, until Jesus walks among men in the days of the New Testament. Moses had an amazing opportunity to represent the people before God and to represent God to the people.

Moses was so close to God that he developed a "holy glow." The people watched him go up to the mountain and into that tent, and they also saw a permanent "mark" on Moses when he returned: There was an actual glow of God in his face! They called the glow "radiant":

> When Moses came down from Mount Sinai with the two tablets of the Testimony in his hands, *he was not aware that his face was radiant because he had spoken with the LORD*. When Aaron and all the Israelites saw Moses, *his face was radiant*, and they were afraid to come near him. But Moses called to them; so Aaron and all the leaders of the community came back to him, and he spoke to them.

Afterward all the Israelites came near him, and he gave them all the commands the LORD had given him on Mount Sinai.

When Moses finished speaking to them, he put a veil over his face. But whenever he entered the LORD's presence to speak with him, he removed the veil until he came out. And when he came out and told the Israelites what he had been commanded, *they saw that his face was radiant.* Then Moses would put the veil back over his face until he went in to speak with the LORD. (Ex. 34:29–35)

We also see a mentoring principal I will describe in the next chapter—"leading to leave." We see in Exodus 33:11 that Joshua was with Moses in the tent. When Moses returned to the camp, often Joshua would stay in the tent. Was he listening for further instructions? Or was he interceding for Moses as he went to the camp and talked with the people? My guess is that both things happened. "God," Joshua might have prayed, "I am not sure they are going to like Moses' words. Help prepare their hearts!" Part of mentoring future leaders has to do with a partnering in prayer.

Here again is this passage where the whole leadership group goes together into the tent of meeting:

The LORD said to Moses: "Bring me seventy of Israel's elders who are known to you as leaders and officials among the people. *Have them come to the Tent of Meeting, that they may stand there with you.* I

> will come down and speak with you there, and I will
> take of the Spirit that is on you and put the Spirit
> on them. They will help you carry the burden of the
> people so that you will not have to carry it alone."
> (Num. 11:16–17)

I love the picture of Moses' leadership team here in Numbers 11, as Moses stood with his leaders, waiting for directions from God. What great instruction for our modern leadership teams! How much time do we spend in God's presence, waiting for His Spirit to wash over us?

Then it occurred to me ... how many of my prayers through the years have been so much more about asking for something rather than about listening? Unfortunately I know the answer to that question. I tend to pray when in crisis. I seek God in the tough times when I need His help. Moses' story taught me to stand still and wait on God. I'm trying to practice his prayer: "If You don't go with us, then we are not moving" (Ex. 33:15, author's paraphrase). We need to practice the art of sitting and listening and being still enough to know that He is God.

My son Jeremy, who is a deeply spiritual man, told me something about this that is quite profound. Isn't it great when our kids sharpen us spiritually? He said, "If you can't be silent in your soul and listen to

> IF YOU CAN'T BE SILENT, THEN ... YOU WILL HAVE NOTHING TO SAY: "BE STILL, AND KNOW THAT I AM GOD; I WILL BE EXALTED AMONG THE NATIONS, I WILL BE EXALTED IN THE EARTH" (PS. 46:10).

God, then you can't be silent in your soul and listen to people. If you can't be silent, then when you open your mouth, you will have nothing to say to man or to God." It was because Moses spent so much time with God that he had so much to say to the people.

WHERE IS YOUR TENT?

In my travels around the world, I have never actually seen a tent of meeting or a tabernacle like the one Moses used. I grew up a Boy Scout and spent a lot of time in camping tents. There are tentlike yurts in Mongolia that might come close. I remember spending an amazing day in a bedouin tent in the desert outside of Dakar, Senegal, with a family enjoying a traditional tea ceremony. We just don't have tabernacles or tents of meeting in our modern time like those built in the time of Moses. And we don't have the temple in Jerusalem anymore either—just the mount. What we do have are many church buildings, and these look vastly different from one country to the next. If you worship in China or Mali, I can assure you that the churches there look very different from our suburban American version. Most churches that meet around the world do not have parking lots or grass, and they generally have less square footage per worshipper than our US churches. I worshipped with a congregation in Mali not long ago where seventy people were packed into a building about the size of my two-car garage. And in Hong Kong, the church I visited met on the fifteenth floor of a high-rise apartment building.

Church buildings are not always the best place to meet God. After all, Jesus said that the kingdom of God would be inside of us: "Once, having been asked by the Pharisees when the kingdom of God would come, Jesus replied, 'The kingdom of God does not come with your careful observation, nor will people say, "Here it is," or "There it is," because the kingdom of God is within you'" (Luke 17:20–21). Personally I know that I struggle to connect with God in church.

So what is the best "tent" for you when it comes to hanging out with God? I think about a beautiful mountain cabin here in Colorado. We have some friends who allow us to use their place from time to time for writing or just relaxing. The week I spent up there by myself writing was a spiritual high. I'm so thankful for the beauty of God's creation. The weather was good and the skies crystal-clear blue. Every day I took a break to ride my mountain bike in Pike National Forest. My favorite route is on a single track lined with aspen and pine trees that cover the path like a canopy. I started thinking about the tent of meeting, which also had a canopy. It struck me one day as I was riding beneath those trees—*Lord, this is my tent!* That bike track is one amazing tent of meeting for me! I feel closest to God and have the most in-depth prayer out in His creation. Yes, my best prayer times are on my bicycle.

> SO WHAT IS THE BEST "TENT" FOR YOU WHEN IT COMES TO HANGING OUT WITH GOD?

Recently, we went to a restaurant with a beautiful outdoor garden patio filled with flowers. I looked down on the ground, and surrounded by pansies was a big rock with these words chiseled into the stone: "You're closer to God's heart in a garden than any place on earth." That might not work for me, but it does for them.

Some shortsighted people probably believe that there is only one right way to experience God, and of course that happens "at church." It kind of reminds me of the Pharisees. They were more concerned with Jesus' wrongful actions on the Sabbath, and the proper use of the temple, than with connecting to the presence of God Himself who walked on the earth. The fact is that there are many ways to worship God and experience His presence. It has a lot to do with our background, our personality, and the traditions to which we have been exposed. In my many years of international travels, I've met a lot of people from a lot of different Christian backgrounds, and I've observed how people connect with God in so many diverse ways. When I attended an Orthodox service recently near our offices here in Littleton, I witnessed a way to connect with God that was a world apart from the traditions that I have known. Is there one right way to connect with God? I think not.

Here are some of the different ways I've observed people connect with God:

> Worship services or just being ...
> In a traditional church
> In a contemporary church
> In a cathedral
> In a small country church
> In a house church
> In a cozy corner in your house with a cup of coffee

In a boat on the water

On a beach, watching a beautiful sunset

In the forest

In the mountains

Anywhere in the great outdoors

In a group

In solitude

Fill in the blank _____

Prayer Is Tough for Me

I began this chapter with my confession that prayer is a tough topic for me to write on because I feel like such a failure. Only pilots should write manuals on how to fly, and only people who pray well and often should write about how to pray. So why is prayer so hard for me? I've been pondering this question for a long time. The other day I attended an all-day prayer summit. No structure, no program, no musicians—just prayer in a room with 150 people as God led us. Actually it was an amazing day, and I do find it easier to focus on prayer in groups than by myself. Maybe it is because Jesus said, "For where two or three gather together as my followers, I am there among them" (Matt. 18:20 NLT). Now, I didn't really look forward to the prayer day ahead of time, I admit it—*in fact, I was dreading the day*. But when it happened, I really enjoyed it.

While I was journaling that day, I came up with a list of the reasons why praying alone is tough for me. Can you relate to any of these? Maybe I got a little carried away with my list—I do that sometimes. But for me this was a great exercise to help me better understand my relationship with God:

1. I am a type A personality. I have a hard time sitting and doing "nothing." Prayer is not "nothing" of course. But for a type A person, it seems like lack of productivity.

2. My family always judged me on what I did (performance)— not who I was becoming (character).

3. I am an INTJ on the Myers-Briggs—introverted and decisive. I thrive on getting things done by myself.

4. I am an ACA—adult child of an alcoholic. This really does affect a person's prayer life. My counselor told me that this means we follow these four rules:

    –Don't talk (about what's important).

    –Don't feel (especially "difficult" emotions).

    –Don't trust (too much danger).

    –Don't stop working (you will never succeed).

5. I am a visual person—as opposed to a verbal person. (Prayer is verbal.)

6. I am a pragmatic German—as opposed to abstract or mystic. (Prayer exists in the immaterial—though I know there are some Germans who were great prayer warriors, like George Mueller).

7. I am not poetic—poetry and the Psalms are not my favorite place to camp.

8. I am a technology freak—I love machines and electronics. They help me get a lot done! But they also distract me away from quietness and reflection.

9. I am a terrible "sitter in meetings." I get very fidgety and restless.

10. And finally—and this is a big one—I was not close to my father. We had a distant, sterile relationship that lacked any warmth or intimacy. I know that we relate to God with the same type of relationship that we had or have with our earthly fathers. For some of us, that is huge and a lot to overcome. I mentioned the great praying woman I married. I see that Donna has such a great intimate relationship to God, in part because she is so very close to her dad.

I have been taught all my life about praying with the "ACTS" formula: Adoration, Confession, Thanksgiving, and Supplication. It seems to me that for most of us, prayer is really about getting around to the "S." We use prayer as God's 911 help line—"Help us, Lord, with this and that problem …"

This change to the "ACTS" formula—what Moses was doing in the tent every day—might be a better way to approach God:

A—Adoration

C—Contemplation

T—Time

S—Silence

In my exposure to followers of the Orthodox Christian tradition, I found that they have an edge over us evangelicals in this arena of time alone with God. Our zeal is to get the word out; their zeal is time in the tent. They believe that we cannot represent God to people until we have spent considerable time with Him. One person told me that their paradigm is "first comes the vertical nourishment by God's grace, and then the horizontal bringing of that nourishment to others." So for the Orthodox believer, prayer is:

> Stop
> Rest
> Contemplate
> Wait on God
> Bring God to people

We could each learn some good things from others. Regardless of our varied traditions, the point of this chapter is that Moses had a rich relationship with God. He walked with God, and that relationship gave him power as a leader. In fact, Moses refused to lead without the presence of God, as we saw at the beginning of this chapter:

> Then Moses said to him, "*If your Presence does not go with us, do not send us up from here.* How will anyone know that you are pleased with me and with your people *unless you go with us?*" (Ex. 33:15–16)

And how did God answer Moses? He said yes. Here is one of my goals as a ministry leader and for my leadership team: that God would be pleased with us, know us by name, and therefore go with us in all that we endeavor.

> And the LORD said to Moses, "I will do the very thing you have asked, because I am pleased with you and I know you by name." (Ex. 33:17)

8

LEADERSHIP COMMANDMENT #8: THOU SHALT LEAD TO LEAVE

Moses said to the LORD, "May the LORD, the God of the
spirits of all mankind, appoint a man over this community
to go out and come in before them, one who will lead them
out and bring them in, so the LORD's people will not be
like sheep without a shepherd." (Num. 27:15–17)

Big Idea: Leadership success without successors is failure. We should lead
not by hanging on to our positions of authority till the bitter end—but
by mentoring future leaders so we leave with grace and open hands.

Do you remember the Klingons in Star Trek? Klingons are a fictional
warrior race in the *Star Trek* universe, and they're not good guys.
They were ugly, and they were bad. It is my contention that some

leaders can be just as bad when they try to "cling on" to their positions too hard and for too long.

I remember hearing that great church consultant Lyle Schaller observe years ago that most leaders stay too long as opposed to leaving too soon. And his corollary comment was this: We do more damage in overstaying our welcome. It's better to leave too soon than to stay too late. Leave while they are still begging you to stay! It reminds me of what my mentor Howard Hendricks taught me in seminary: "Less is more when communicating in public speaking. The best talks leave the audience wanting more. Stop talking before the audience stops listening." So I guess the corollary for leadership is that we should *stop leading before our followers stop following*. He who thinks he's leading but finds that no one is following is just taking a walk.

> HE WHO THINKS HE'S LEADING BUT FINDS THAT NO ONE IS FOLLOWING IS JUST TAKING A WALK.

ALL IN OR ALL GONE

In recent months, I have decided it is time for me to step down as the leader of our ministry. I have asked the board to begin the succession plan to find my replacement. The number one issue for me has been my own heart. My heart is no longer fully engaged in my job. As we will see in the next chapter, matters of the heart are the biggest issues of all when contemplating career decisions. I realized that as the leader I have to be *all in or all gone*. Leaders need to leave when their passion has departed. I came to a place in my own leadership where I could no longer give it my all. The passion and the challenge of the assignment had truly left the building. God is calling me to new horizons, and I need to make the hard decision to leave my current assignment. It is not fair to my organization or to me personally for me to stay in leadership when the fire has gone out of my heart.

In the analogy of Moses, I have fought my share of giants, and I have no more to give. I can clearly see the next giants facing our future, but I have lost the heart to fight them. I have a clear sense that it is time for the Joshuas and Calebs to take over. When you have no passion left to solve the problems facing your organization's future, you have to make way for the next generation of problem solvers. That is what I refer to as the final act of good leadership. It has become very clear to me that I cannot sit on the fence as a leader. Tentative leadership kills the spirit of the whole organization. People were sensing that I was drifting away, but it was up to me to do something about it. How many churches and ministries are stalled by a leader who is all used up but refuses to let go? I do not want to be one of those leaders who overstays his welcome. It's better to leave too soon than to stay too long.

The one thing we all have to face sooner or later is the question of finishing well. Not one of us will stay in our assignments forever. Just like death and taxes, it is certain that there is a beginning and an end to every ministry assignment. For every Moses, there will come a time for a Joshua.

It seems to me that starting a new leadership assignment is the easy part, when compared to finishing well. We usually begin any new leadership challenge with vision, passion, and enthused expectancy. But what about the other end? How do we feel when we see our days of leadership assignment coming to a close? We sense that things are winding down, and we have to leave without hurting the organization. The time of departure for any leader can be a very destructive time, and sadly, few leaders depart as well as they start.

When it comes time for a leader to finish, there is usually a need to find a replacement. That is when the white water of succession planning gets rough. Simply put, a succession plan is *the orderly handover of a leadership position from the outgoing leader to the incoming leader, including the selection and orientation of the right replacement.* Many a church and many a ministry has failed miserably and had huge setbacks by failing in this transition. What causes this failure? A long list of challenges during leadership transition: poorly run search teams, differing visions about who the new leaders should be, picking the wrong replacement, internal power struggles, politics, panic, and just plain incompetency. My advice for any organization in leadership transition is to get professional help and take your time to get it right. If the former leader is gone, appoint an interim while you take the time to get it right.

Leading with the attitude of leaving is not about disengaging in leadership like a lame duck. *Not at all.* Rather, it is about a spirit of humility and knowing that you are replaceable. It's wise to hold the ministry of leadership with open hands, praying, "Lord, help me not to be a cling-on." Be aware that God gave the position of leadership, and He can also choose to take it away. Be willing to walk away and make room for Joshua just as Moses did. For me, I want to finish the way that Moses did. Moses was Joshua's champion, and he didn't cling to his authority at the end. He was not mad at God for denying him entrance to the Promised Land. Once God told Moses that he was done, Moses prayed for his successor and sought for him aggressively: "Moses said to the LORD, 'May the LORD, the God of the spirits of all mankind, appoint a man over this community to go out and come in before them, one who will lead them out and bring them in, so the LORD's people will not be like sheep without a shepherd'" (Num. 27:15–17).

I know that there's a promised land for the future of our organization that I will not experience. I'm okay with that. Great things will happen in the future that I will not be a part of, and I want to leave the ministry in as good a shape as possible as I hand it off to the next generation. That will be my final act of leadership in this assignment.

Warren Webster, my predecessor, taught me how to lead to leave. As I've mentioned before in other books, when I became president of WorldVenture, we were a fifty-year-old organization, and I was part of an amazingly orderly leadership transition. I look back two decades later and still have great admiration for the humility of the man who went before me. My predecessor finished well by focusing on the future even though he knew he wouldn't be a part of it. In effect, he asked me to take us into the promised land of my generation.

While I was in the final process of being selected as CEO, I vividly recall one statement Warren made to me: "Success without a successor is failure." He honestly believed this principle and lived it out by allowing for a smooth and orderly transfer of power. And he walked away from a twenty-three-year run as a very strong CEO.

I remember asking him, "How can I ever fill your shoes?" He smiled and said, "I don't want you to. I am taking my shoes with me! You need to be your own man." Warren has gone on to his reward with Jesus, but one of the last things he told me before he died was this: "I believe that the best days for WorldVenture lie in the future!" That attitude is not clinging on— rather it's evidence of a big, open heart. It takes a big person to leave in this way and say that we will do better things than he did. Do you know how motivating that perspective was to me as a young leader? It will soon be my turn to model that kind of attitude.

> "SUCCESS WITHOUT A SUCCESSOR IS FAILURE."
> —WARREN WEBSTER

Moses knew that he would not enter the Promised Land—he grasped the reality we all have to face as leaders: There will be a day when we no longer lead. The day has come for me to step away from my position. Okay, I admit, when we are young, we don't often think of leaving or of the next step. But transition happens all the time in leadership positions. Sometimes transition is brought on by retirement, but often it's just leadership turnover. I just met this week with one of our directors who plans to retire in four years, and we reviewed the names of possible candidates who could replace him. He has given it a lot of thought, and that effort is very helpful to those of us who will have to choose the next person for that slot.

Moses asked God to find his replacement. Great idea! That is a good prayer model for every leader: "Lord, help me identity those

young emerging leaders who are coming up behind me." God
answered the prayer and identified Joshua and then asked Moses to
empower him:

> So the LORD said to Moses, *"Take Joshua son of*
> *Nun, a man in whom is the spirit, and lay your hand*
> *on him.* Have him stand before Eleazar the priest
> and the entire assembly and commission him in
> their presence. *Give him some of your authority so*
> *the whole Israelite community will obey him."* (Num.
> 27:18–20)

It worked! The spirit that resided in Moses was passed on to
Joshua: "Now Joshua son of Nun was filled with the spirit of wisdom because Moses had laid his hands on him. So the Israelites
listened to him and did what the LORD had commanded Moses"
(Deut. 34:9).

This is great example of a successful leadership transfer. For forty
years Moses looked forward to finally taking his people into the
Promised Land. But it was not to be. His successor, Joshua, fulfilled
Moses' dream. In fact, the day before he died, Moses was shown the
Promised Land and told that his descendants would possess it but
that he would never set foot in it: "I have let you see it with your eyes,
but you will not cross over into it" (Deut. 34:4).

How did Moses handle the truth that his successor would have
greater success than he, and that Joshua would actually fulfill the
objectives Moses himself had sought to achieve for forty years? He
handled it with godly grace and dignity.

How Moses supported the leader who would
replace him:

He believed in Joshua.

He mentored Joshua.

He prayed for Joshua.

He empowered Joshua by laying his hands on
him.

He supported Joshua publicly in front of the
people.

He cast vision for Joshua's future leadership
success.

He stepped back and allowed Joshua to take over.

JOSHUA TO SUCCEED MOSES

My absolute favorite passage about leadership transition from the
story of Moses is found in Deuteronomy 31. When I read these
verses describing how Joshua would succeed Moses, I see one of
the great biblical examples of leadership transition done right. Just
look at the spirit of Moses as he champions the young up-and-
comer Joshua:

> Then Moses went out and spoke these words to
> all Israel: "I am now a hundred and twenty years
> old and I am no longer able to lead you. The LORD
> has said to me, 'You shall not cross the Jordan.' The

LORD your God himself will cross over ahead of you. He will destroy these nations before you, and you will take possession of their land. *Joshua also will cross over ahead of you,* as the LORD said. And the LORD will do to them what he did to Sihon and Og, the kings of the Amorites, whom he destroyed along with their land. The LORD will deliver them to you, and you must do to them all that I have commanded you. Be strong and courageous. Do not be afraid or terrified because of them, for the LORD your God goes with you; he will never leave you nor forsake you."

Then Moses summoned Joshua and said to him in the presence of all Israel, "Be strong and courageous, for you must go with this people into the land that the LORD swore to their forefathers to give them, and you must divide it among them as their inheritance. The LORD himself goes before you and will be with you; he will never leave you nor forsake you. Do not be afraid; do not be discouraged." (Deut. 31:1–8)

The plan worked, the transition was smooth, and the followers immediately transferred their allegiance to Joshua. Moses in humility placed his hands on Joshua and prayed for God's blessing on his leadership. That is a picture of leadership maturity in the final hour, when it probably counts the most. Do you realize how often this does not happen?

Barriers to Grooming Your Successor

Many leaders do not leave well when their time is done. The Moses-to-Joshua handover is rare today. Whether it is their own initiative to move on, as in my case, or being asked to leave, many don't have a good track record of leaving well. Sadly, great leadership legacy can be spoiled in these final months before departure. I think our egos get in the way. The outgoing leader might think no one else could become as good as he or she was: "I am the father of this family—how can anyone take my place?" The best thing we can do for our legacy as we are on our way out is to set aside our egos and make the way as smooth and supportive as possible to the one coming in to replace us.

As I just mentioned, my board recently launched the formal succession of my leadership to find my replacement. They asked me to stay on for a smooth transition until that successor is identified. My colleagues and I are all committed to my finishing well. It occurred to me that strong leadership through this transition will be my final ultimate leadership contribution, since so many leaders do not finish well and do not depart well. I would love to have the transition out of my leadership as smooth as when I came in under Warren Webster. Like two great bookends to the two decades of my leadership. It reminds me of the words of Max Lucado: "Your last chapters can be your best. Your final song can be your greatest. It could be that all of your life has prepared you for a grand exit."[1]

Let me get very real about this process: I'm facing it myself. It is easy to talk about the business of passing the baton, but it can be painful in reality. As I look over this list of barriers, I realize that every one of them is real for me. If you're in the same place that I am, facing a leadership transition soon, ask yourself how many of these barriers you will face:

> Identity and self-worth—I am what I do
>
> What am I going to do next?
>
> Fear of retirement
>
> Fear of transition
>
> Resistance to change
>
> The saddle is so comfortable
>
> This role is my whole life
>
> Lack of confidence
>
> Arrogance—who else can do this job?
>
> Love for the job
>
> Love for the leadership role
>
> Loss of investment
>
> I've put too much into this group to let it go

I'm so thankful that Warren overcame this list of barriers and transferred his role to me when it was time for him to retire. At the same time that this was happening to me, a good friend of mine was also installed as the president and CEO of a large international organization. But while his experience and mine were simultaneous, we had dramatically different results. His transition was a disaster. The leader preceding my friend Bill (not his real name) sabotaged his transition. Even though the predecessor knew he had to retire and leave, he made life miserable and difficult for Bill.

First of all, the departing leader went throughout the organization promising everyone that there would be no changes in leadership or staff. He actually made that announcement publicly at his retirement dinner in the presence of all the significant leaders of the organization. He also told everyone that there would be no dramatic changes in strategy or direction. In effect he told everyone, "Bill is going to pick up where I left off and do things the way I've done them." *Gee, thanks for the handcuffs!* How different that is from what Moses did in the passage we just read from Deuteronomy 31, which essentially says, "Go and take the land and do it your way!"

The actions of this retiring leader were the opposite of letting go. This former leader was so self-absorbed that he couldn't imagine someone else stepping in and leading the organization in a different way. This retiring leader thought he could continue leading into the future *through Bill.* He did a lot of harm to the organization, and as a result, my friend Bill lasted only a couple of years. He was smart enough to leave and went on to a much better situation. As I watched the story play out, I knew that Bill would not survive. We often compared notes during those early days of our leadership. Talking to Bill made me even more thankful for all the support I received publicly and privately from Dr. Webster.

Bill became what is known as the *unintentional interim.* Many times interim leaders follow strong leaders to become a buffer between the last strong leader and the next. As I think about my own transition, I want to do everything I can to avoid being followed by an interim leader who has to clean up a transition mess.

As I write these words, I think of my good friend Jerry Rankin, who recently retired as the president of the International Mission

Board of the Southern Baptist Convention. He led that mission through tremendous change for seventeen years. He led well, finished well, and did an exemplary job of *leading to leave.*

Jerry and I became good friends in May 1993, when we both concurrently began our responsibilities as presidents of our respective ministries. Even though his organization was ten times larger than ours, we had a lot in common and have enjoyed tremendous camaraderie over these years. I highly recommend to you one of his latest books: *Spiritual Warfare: The Battle for God's Glory.* Recently I wrote Jerry and asked him to reflect on his departure after seventeen years. His comments fit so well in this chapter:

> As a leader approaches the conclusion of his tenure, I think the most important element to finishing well is to position the organization for the future. Real leaders readily understand that the mark of leadership is not what is accomplished during one's tenure, statistical growth, or bottom-line profits, but whether or not one's style of leadership and strategic decisions have positioned the organization for even greater growth and success in the future. That means having created truly a vision-driven organization that continues to stay focused on the task, creating a structure and a top echelon of leadership that will sustain the vision and strategy that has been set in place, and, where possible actually mentoring and nurturing a successor that is the obvious one to inherit the mantle of leadership. One

can be immensely successful in their leadership, but
if all they have accomplished comes screeching to
a halt once they are no longer in place, they have
obviously not finished well![2]

Empowering the Emerging Generations

The leaders who replace us will be more different than ever. I have to
think differently about the emerging twenty- and thirtysomethings,
because they are growing up in a very different reality.

One of my priorities as a leader is the mentoring of our emerging
leadership pool. As often as possible, I ask myself: *Who are our future
leaders? Who are the people I am targeting and developing for future leadership? Where are the men and women who will lead us next?* This is not
playing favorites; rather it is preparing for our organization's future.

If success without a successor is failure, then I must groom the
men and women who will take my place. I keep a running list on my
laptop of the promising leaders who will pick up where I leave off. I
also have a list for every one of the key leaders around me who will
transition out in the next five or so years. I ask them each to keep me
posted with the names of three to five people within our organization
who could take their place if they were run over by a bus tomorrow. I
look them over and think, *Yes, he could become director of this. She will
be ready for that role in a few years.* In fact, sometimes as I speak to our
younger staff members, I look into their faces and think to myself, *One*

of you might replace me! That thought excites me and motivates me to pave the way for them. They are not a threat but rather the ultimate completion of my leadership. Do you have your lists in the works?

Over the last five years I implemented a president's intern program, so that young leaders could shadow me for a year. I consider the participants a part of our leadership pipeline, so they might as well learn the challenges firsthand from me now. My intern program is really about mentoring future leaders for *any* leadership slot within WorldVenture. It's an informal program, and it doesn't have a whole lot of structure, but it requires a lot of time. Inclusion in the program is not a declaration that they might replace me. Rather, it's a statement that we think they show great promise for the future of our ministry.

My theory is that I just need to spend time with my interns. It is an organic process. These interns are people in our organization who over a period of one year have special access to me. They travel with me. They are included in most leadership meetings. They actually get to sit in our board of directors meetings. We go on bike rides together. If they're married, we enjoy social connections with our spouses and children. We drink a lot of coffee together at Starbucks. To me it's a Paul-and-Timothy kind of relationship. Not only am I seeking to develop future leaders with my own personal time and input, but I am also modeling this behavior for the other leaders in our organization. I want them to do the same with other up-and-coming leaders on their teams.

Organizations live and die on the basis of their flow of new leadership talent. The only way to guarantee that our ministries

> ORGANIZATIONS LIVE AND DIE ON THE BASIS OF THEIR FLOW OF NEW LEADERSHIP TALENT.

do not slide down into institutionalization, calcification, bureau-
cracy, and death is to constantly renew our organizations with fresh
blood in the form of new leaders.

Who knows what might happen to us along the way?

Clyde McDowell was a dear friend of mine in the late 1990s.
He was the promising young new president at Denver Seminary.
One of the reasons we moved our home office operations to Denver
was to partner side by side with Clyde as the seminary prepared
students for global outreach. No sooner did we get relocated to
Colorado than Clyde developed a brain tumor, and he died six
months later—at just forty-nine years of age. This taught me again
how quickly our leadership can end and how important it is to
lead with a team. The good news about Clyde is that his dream
for a seminary with a strong emphasis on mentoring has become a
reality ten years later.

I am optimistic about the up-and-coming generations. While
some people are worried, the next generations inspire me. I see a
lot of them more serious about changing the world than my own
generation. I want to finish this chapter by covering some of the
positive characteristics that I see in young people today. This list
might apply to many people in America under forty years of age.
I am very excited about these young new leaders. Sure, there's a lot
of self-centeredness in some young people today—but isn't that a
trait of all young people through the decades? I meet a lot of young
people today who want to make a difference. They are not skeptical
but engaging. The only downside of their passion is that our instant
electronic culture has made them impatient: They want to change
the world by Friday afternoon!

The Top Ten Traits of Young People Coming into Leadership in Ministries and Churches

1. Long for a sense of belonging
2. Value authenticity, transparency, and humility
3. View conversion as journey rather than destination
4. Integrate the Great Commission with the Great Commandment
5. Function best with flat and fluid leadership structures
6. Focus on their microstory, not one big macrostory
7. Admire kingdom thinkers—not empire builders
8. Find meaning in ambiguity, paradox, metaphor, mystery, and creativity
9. Expect/demand meaningful engagement
10. Interpret Scripture as the story of God's redemptive purpose rather than the repository of propositional truth

We have to always have one eye on our replacements. Not in a threatened way, but to ensure the long-term success of the enterprise we lead. Instead of being "cling-ons," let's move forward as we find our Joshuas, mentor them, and celebrate their leadership.

For you who are reading these words and are a part of that new generation, look for mentors and leaders who will give you room to grow. Look for your Moses with humility, and ask older leaders to take you under their wings for a season.

9

LEADERSHIP COMMANDMENT #9: THOU SHALT NEVER GIVE UP

I cannot carry all these people by myself; the burden is too heavy for me. If this is how you are going to treat me, put me to death right now—if I have found favor in your eyes—and do not let me face my own ruin. (Num. 11:14–15)

Big Idea: There are many times we want to quit as leaders. There is not a leader alive who will not face deep waters of loneliness and discouragement. It is lonely at the top. This chapter will explore why that is true and why we need to be patient in leadership.

I almost quit my job at just the time I was not supposed to, and I am so glad that I didn't. I've learned deep lessons about career discouragements that I need to share here. I know you will find them useful.

Sometimes the exact right move is to quit. My friend Craig is selling his business in Los Angeles and is moving to China to do student ministry with Chinese students. In his case, he had all the right reasons to leave a rut and follow the adventurous call of God. His business lost money in recent years, and his heart is no longer in it. I took him on a vision trip to China, and the next thing you know—God grabbed his heart for a new adventure!

Another friend of mine recently resigned as the pastor of a megachurch in Minnesota. The people loved him and he loved them, and it was a church and position with a lot of prestige. But his heart was no longer in the assignment. It was not a failure of any kind, nor did the members want him to leave. He had just had a dream to pursue a specialized ministry for prayer full-time. I applaud my friend for following his dream. He jumped off the diving board and into the deep end of faith to follow his dream. There are times when quitting is exactly the right thing to do.

But what happens when we quit for the wrong reasons? When we throw in the towel out of discouragement because we can't take it anymore? Could it be that just around the corner we'll find success? Here are some famous failures who refused to quit, and I think we would all agree that it was a good thing they did not:

Dismissed from drama school with a note that read, "Wasting her time. She's too shy to put her best foot forward."—Lucille Ball

Fired from a newspaper because he "lacked imagination and had no original ideas."—Walt Disney

Turned down by the Decca recording company, who said, "We don't like their sound, and guitar music is on the way out."—The Beatles

A failed soldier, farmer, and real-estate agent. At thirty-eight years old he went to work for his father as a handyman.—Ulysses S. Grant

Cut from his high school basketball team, he went home and locked himself in his room and cried. —Michael Jordan

His teacher told him he was too stupid to learn anything and that he should go into a field where he could succeed by virtue of his pleasant personality.—Thomas Edison

His fiancée died. He failed in business twice. He had a nervous breakdown and was defeated in eight elections.—Abraham Lincoln[1]

So when was the first time Moses wanted to quit? He wanted to quit after the first conversation with God at the burning bush—we reviewed all his excuses in chapter 2. Then of course he wanted to quit when Pharaoh would not let his people go. That rejection was really tough, and I don't think he saw it coming!

Moses probably thought, *Wait a minute, God—I am doing* exactly *what You asked me to do, and it is not working.* That's not in the Bible—it's just what I believe he was thinking. Certainly Moses wanted to resign when the people whined for water and food and asked to go back to Egypt. I have no doubt he was frustrated when he came down from his forty days up on Mount Sinai and threw the tablets at his rebellious followers during the golden calf incident.

There is not a leader alive who will not face the deep waters of loneliness and discouragement. It is lonely at the top. It is not about having a thick skin but about protecting our hearts from despair. I have opened my heart to some people about the great doubt and discouragement I've faced in my leadership. In this chapter I will open the curtain and show you some of what I went through.

Moses' Darkest Hour

In the story of Moses, what would you say was the most discouraging day in his life? I think of two. The first was the day he came down from the mountain with the tablets to find his followers worshiping a golden calf. Fortunately, Moses did not quit on that day. The second day is recorded in Numbers 11, when Moses complained to God most adamantly about his leadership burden.

This scene begins with scorched earth. There is so much anger from God against the ceaseless whining of the people that He shoots fire down from above and kills some of the Israelites. Okay, admit it. You have wished for this at some point in your leadership career.

> Now the people complained about their hardships in
> the hearing of the LORD, and when he heard them his

anger was aroused. Then fire from the LORD burned
among them and consumed some of the outskirts of
the camp. When the people cried out to Moses, he
prayed to the LORD and the fire died down. So that
place was called Taberah, because fire from the LORD
had burned among them. (Num. 11:1–3)

As I mentioned earlier, *discouragement* can be the number one
tool in Satan's arsenal to take out leaders. If he hates what we're
doing, he will try everything to bring us down. I have found such
encouragement in seeing how much pressure Moses faced and yet
kept going. Here we read the rawest account yet of the burned-out,
wounded heart of Moses complaining to God about the people he
is asked to lead:

Moses heard the people of every family wailing,
each at the entrance to his tent. The LORD became
exceedingly angry, *and Moses was troubled.* He asked
the LORD, "Why have you brought this trouble on
your servant? What have I done to displease you that
you put the burden of all these people on me? Did
I conceive all these people? Did I give them birth?
Why do you tell me to carry them in my arms, as a
nurse carries an infant, to the land you promised on
oath to their forefathers?" (Num. 11:10–12)

This was the breaking point for Moses. He actually asked God to
take his life: "I cannot carry all these people by myself; the burden is

too heavy for me. If this is how you are going to treat me, put me to death right now—if I have found favor in your eyes—and do not let me face my own ruin" (Num. 11:14–15).

Have people ever made you feel this way? Have you ever come to this breaking point? You will if you haven't yet. I have been there and done that. The prayer of Moses has on occasion become my prayer: "Lord, are these my children? Did I bring them into the world? Why have you asked *me* to lead *them?* Can't you find me some more well-behaved people to lead? Or will you release me, and find someone else suitable to lead them?" Please don't misunderstand my words here. I lead great people. It's just that the burden of the problems and disputes that arise among them can get overwhelming. People are messy, and those messes—especially the messes that can drag on for months without resolution—get very draining at times.

Discouragement in leadership has many sources beyond the complaining of followers. Discouragement can come in many other forms that weigh on the hearts of leaders. What can you not carry anymore? When can you no longer bear the burden? What are you carrying that is wearing you out?

> Loneliness—no life partner
> Deadly disease in your family
> Divided church
> Lack of growth
> Stagnation and boredom
> Resistant board
> Troublesome staff
> Unrealistic demands on your life

Financial failure

Exhaustion

Rebellious child

Empty marriage

Leaders must be purveyors of hope. That gets hard at times when our own hope gets shaky. In Numbers 11 we see just such a moment for Moses. I think it was his darkest hour and most hopeless moment. Hope is the faith factor inside of us that believes we will realize our dreams. When everyone else loses hope, we as leaders have to keep that hope alive. We don't quit when everyone else around us is ready to. Moses kept fanning the flames of faith when everyone gave up on Canaan and wanted to go back to Egypt. Winston Churchill was right when he said: "Never give in—never, never, never, in nothing, great or small, large or petty; never give in except to convictions of honor and good sense."

> WHEN EVERYONE ELSE LOSES HOPE, WE AS LEADERS HAVE TO KEEP HOPE ALIVE. WE DON'T QUIT WHEN EVERYONE ELSE IS READY TO.

IS IT TIME TO LEAVE?

I meet a lot of leaders who want to quit because they cannot get their people to change. Perhaps you're asking yourself these questions: *Can I really make a difference? Or should I just move on?*

I regularly get letters and emails from people who ask me that very question: "Here is the situation I am in. What is your recommendation? Should I try to bring about change, is there any hope that things will be different, or should I just bail out and find a group that's more satisfying to work with?" I usually try to encourage people to stick with it ... up to a point. If they don't see any movement or any responsiveness to suggestions for change, it's probably best to move on.

Many times people ask me, "To what point do I hang in there? How long do I keep trying before I give up and go elsewhere?" Below are a few guidelines to help answer that critical question, "Is it time to leave?" I would say it is time to go if several of these things are present:

- Too much broken glass on the floor—you or your team has done too many things wrong to set things back in order. Too much broken trust and lack of respect exist and cannot be repaired.
- You are not the leader and have lost faith in the leadership above you; personal or professional integrity has been compromised. You can no longer accept the actions of your leader or fellow leaders in good conscience. A great resource on this topic is the book *Integrity* by Henry Cloud.
- You're working in less than 25 percent of your area of gifting. You are not suited to the responsibilities, and there is no joy in your work.
- Loss of faith and respect from your leader or your board—they are not on the same page and thwart

you at every turn. They have lost trust in your leadership.

- The juice is no longer worth the squeeze. The frustration level is much greater than the opportunities if things did change. You don't have any good weeks—just one bad week after another.

- People see you as the source of problems. People see you as nothing but a complainer with your continual attempts to push change, and as a result, you carry around a negative cloud in the organization.

- Contract commitments are completed, and you are free to go. Assignment completed.

- Great new opportunities knock on your door. Your heart is being drawn to a new place of leadership that matches who you are.

- The biggest one of all: *Your heart is just not in it anymore. You have lost the passion for the assignment. The challenge has left the building.*

The last item on this list is huge. As I mentioned in the last chapter, it was this one that finally convinced me that it was time to leave. A dear friend of mine encouraged me during this time of wrestling about leaving my position: "You should think about moving if what you see in the rearview mirror (memories) is greater than what's in your view out the front windshield (dreams)."[2] This was so true for me after leading hard for two decades. I am proud of the body of my work and what God accomplished through me. But when it came to the future, I could no longer get excited or passionate looking out our organizational windshield.

THE MYTH OF THE SWEET SPOT—IS THERE LEADERSHIP NIRVANA?

Over the last two weeks I've been sucked dry by a leadership crisis that I did not create but have had to manage. It has to do with confronting staff for relational failures. This is not in my sweet spot. Do any of you reading this really *like* to confront people with bad news about their poor behavior? Not their results *but their behavior*. Not only is it *not* my sweet spot, but it is in fact my *sour spot*—the thing I like doing least. The details of this story are not important; you know what I am talking about. We all have to do things we don't like as part of our leadership roles. It's not that sweet spots don't exist for leaders; I just think that very few people have the privilege of working in their sweet spots full-time. I do think I experience seasons of being in my sweet spot, but those seasons come and go.

I define a sweet spot this way: *working in the perfect leadership assignment where all my gifts and talents are used fully in my job description and I get to spend my days doing what I love.* Sounds like leadership nirvana, right? The sweet spot is a great ideal, but I am not sure it is entirely biblical. Consider what I covered in chapter 2 about *not serving our own ego,* and chapter 3 about *servant leadership.* Being a good leader sometimes requires us to do things we don't like to do as part of our tasks.

The other day I was putting on my baseball cap that is made by the "Life is Good" folks. As I was about to place it on my head, I noticed that sewn inside the cap were the words *Do what you like, like what you do*. God was speaking to me from this hat! That should be our pursuit as we find the right place for our leadership gifts.

I do think we need to find jobs that fit us, but I consider the 60/40 rule a good one: I spend at least 60 percent of my time doing things that I am good at and that are in my gifting area, and I enjoy those things. The other 40 percent is servant leadership—doing those things that have to be done whether I enjoy them or not.

Do you like meetings? I generally hate them. Maybe hate is too strong a word—it's just that they bore me and drain me. I like being productive, and I am an introvert. Add those two ingredients together, and I prefer to work on my own and get things done. Most of the time, meetings kill all that, as we try to work together in a group. It kind of reminds me of junior high when teachers forced us to do projects as a group with other classmates. And that worked out real well. Even if I am in charge, I don't enjoy meetings. I guess it is the introvert in me—and my penchant toward tasks; I have a hard time seeing progress in my work when I am in a meeting all day long. This week I spent most of the week in meetings, and on one day, I never came out of my conference room as I met with one group after another, dealing with this high-level leadership crisis to which I alluded. After the week was over I thought to myself, *Okay, that is not what I signed up for*. But if you don't like meetings, then get out of leadership! This is the 40 percent side of servant leadership that I have to do as a good leader—even though it's not my preferred way to spend my day.

I am a huge fan of personality tests like the Myers-Briggs, which has helped me learn a lot about myself. The results have also helped my colleagues understand why I behave as I do. I have also benefited from what is known as the "StrengthsFinder" inventory. Go to www.strengthsfinder.com to take your own assessment of your strengths. The philosophy behind the StrengthsFinder and the books on the topic follow this philosophy of gifting: "Do you have the opportunity to do what you do best *every day?* Chances are, you don't. All too often, our natural talents go untapped. From the cradle to the cubicle, we devote more time to fixing our shortcomings than to developing our strengths."[3]

The idea behind this inventory is to find out what you are really good at and to help you try to spend more of your time doing whatever that is. This would be working in your sweet spot. To help people uncover their talents, Gallup introduced the first version of its online assessment in the 2001 management book *Now, Discover Your Strengths*, which has been updated in the book *StrengthsFinder 2.0*. Both books spent many months on the best-seller lists, and StrengthsFinder Inventory has helped millions discover their top five talents. Here is my list after taking the assessment:

STRENGTHSFINDER ANALYSIS FOR HANS FINZEL

STRATEGIC

People who are especially talented in the Strategic theme create alternative ways to proceed. Faced with any given scenario, they can quickly spot the relevant patterns and issues.

FUTURISTIC

People who are especially talented in the Futuristic theme are inspired by the future and what could be. They inspire others with their visions of the future.

RELATOR

People who are especially talented in the Relator theme enjoy close relationships with others. They find deep satisfaction in working hard with friends to achieve a goal.

ACHIEVER

People who are especially talented in the Achiever theme have a great deal of stamina and work hard. They take great satisfaction from being busy and productive.

POSITIVITY

People who are especially talented in the Positivity theme have an enthusiasm that is contagious. They are upbeat and can get others excited about what they are going to do.

MY DARKEST DAYS SO FAR

Now it's time for me to pull back the curtain on my darkest moment of discouragement so far in my leadership journey.

A decade ago, the chairman of my board of directors decided it was time to get rid of me for less-than-honorable reasons. When that did not work—because my board did not follow his lead but ousted him instead—he wrote a very painful public letter to hundreds of people in our network, accusing me of actions and beliefs that were simply not true. Never once did he talk to me about these things face-to-face. It seems to me that he very much took a coward's road.

You know the saddest part of this whole story? He was a dear personal friend before all this happened, and I discovered that wounds from a friend are painful. It hurt me deeply. When I was a little kid, we always said on the playground, "Sticks and stones can break my bones, but words will never hurt me." How crazy is that untruth? *Words have the power to devastate!*

The good news is that the people who received the letter had enough good sense to see through the lies. They considered the source, and most did not take it seriously. Unfortunately, some did take it seriously, and that created a rift that lasts till today. The good news was, as I noted earlier, my board sided with me and tossed out the chairman—it sounds pretty painless, but the process played out over many months before we reached resolution. In the midst of these attacks, many other discouraging things happened that led me to want to give up. Without a doubt those were my most disheartening days so far.

As I mentioned in the preface, I actually wrote my resignation letter around that time. It was a great catharsis to get the words out on paper. I highly recommend the exercise just to process emotions. Just don't send it unless you mean it.

These events happened almost a decade ago, and today, I'm so glad I didn't leave at that time. I'm sure there are a few people who were disappointed that I never sent that letter. But many people since have affirmed my leadership as I've continued on. My board has been my greatest encouragement as it stood with me and protected my back.

That night was darkest right before the dawn. I could not agree more with the words of Thomas Edison that I cited in my preface: "Many of life's failures are people who did not realize how close they were to success when they gave up."

Why didn't I leave? As I shared in the beginning of this book, I was studying the leadership of Moses during those days, and that study was just the "aha" that I needed. God's whisper to me in those dark days was: *"Just be faithful and get through each week. I am not yet ready to release you from this assignment."* I was not supposed to bail out just because times were tough. If Moses could handle his problems, certainly I could handle my own far-less-dramatic problems.

Moses begged God to put him out of his misery, like a wounded soldier on a war-weary battlefield. How did God resolve this prayer of Moses? Did He kill him or relieve the pressure? *Neither.* God asked him to build a team and mentor it to share the load. God gave Moses seventy elders to share the burden of leadership, and God gave me many great colleagues to share my load. The clouds of despair cleared away. Things got a whole lot better. It just took some time to get there!

THE GRASS IS NOT GREENER — YOU ARE LIVING NORMALLY

There is a great tension in many leaders about the topic of staying or leaving, and for many of us, there are no clear, easy answers. I've tried to balance both sides of the issue. In my three decades of experience in leadership, I have observed many leaders who felt stuck in a leadership role that only partially motivates them. Stuck with a group of fickle followers for whom they don't really care. Stuck financially in a situation they are unable to get themselves out of. These leaders often end up looking for a new job. They start reading the want ads or surfing the job sites, hoping for a way out. And sometimes, that is the best choice.

My friend Steve tried to lead a church in California that chewed him up and spit him out. I've never heard of a group of followers nastier than the people in this church who ran a good man out of town. In his case, he needed to leave for the sake of his own sanity and the preservation of his family. But for many others, leaving is not the best option when times are tough.

The grass is rarely greener on the other side. You may think other leaders have a better situation than you do, but you are probably wrong. Leadership is about ups and downs. Every leader has headaches. Every leader has days that he or she wants to quit. I respect leaders who work their way through the difficult challenges and problems and don't quit. I don't claim to be a great leader, not by any means. But I am the kind of leader who sticks with the task. Though I have always seen myself as a maverick, I am loyal to the core. And the older I get, the more I value those traits of endurance, faithfulness, and loyalty to a calling. Not very hip or trendy—*but quite biblical!*

There is something admirable about leaders who endure for the long haul. In a recent article about great American companies with amazing track records of stock-value increases, three were singled out because their founders stayed on: Steve Jobs at Apple (he left but came back and revolutionized seven industries including cell phones, music, and computers before his untimely death), Michael Dell at Dell, and Jeff Bezos at Amazon. Their leadership has endured the test of time, and they've built wildly successful long-haul companies. They won't be leading their companies forever, but they have built great companies with patient leadership over a span of more than fifteen years. In today's world, fifteen years in one job is a lifetime! Moses eventually turned over the "company" to Joshua and Caleb, and Dell, Jobs, and Bezos are certainly grooming their replacements as well.

COPING MECHANISMS WHEN YOU ARE OVERWHELMED

The last things I want to talk about in this chapter are coping mechanisms. How do you handle your discouragements in leadership? I've heard leaders suggest that the way to manage resistance, discouragement, and criticism is to develop a thick skin. Boy, I tried that when I was a young leader, and it sure didn't work for me. I think some people like Donald Trump are just born with thick skin. But not me, and not most of the leaders I talk to. As recently as last week I received some harsh criticism. I really take criticism personally. I internalize it and beat myself up about it. I definitely do not have a thick skin.

> DEVELOPING A COARSE EMOTIONAL HIDE IS THE WORST THING YOU COULD POSSIBLY DO AS A LEADER.

As the years went on, I decided that developing a coarse emotional hide is the worst thing you could possibly do as a leader. Making yourself impervious to pain means shutting yourself off from most of the nuances and intricacies of life—and business or ministry as well. I've seen leaders become thick-skinned and insulated before, and it only led to their demise. Before long, they become so well insulated that they cannot hear the whispers of common sense, interpersonal resentment, or even approaching trouble. For a leader, whose greatest responsibility is to sense how the proverbial wind is blowing, that is the kiss of death. Leaders have to be great listeners who are not insulated from constructive feedback.

Rather than develop a thick hide, you can do some of the following things when criticism comes. When someone resists or criticizes you, put into practice some habits that I developed over the years. I guess you could say I've learned to absorb the blows, not deflect them. Instead of trying to develop ways of never feeling the attack, work on ways of processing the attacks in a better way.

FIND CONFIDANTS WHO ARE NOT COLLEAGUES

I absolutely believe in the notion that it is "lonely at the top." What that means to me is that no one can understand the unique pressures that I face as the person in charge of my particular organization. I have pressure from above, pressure from my board, and pressure from everyone below me in the organization itself. The person at the top carries everyone on his or her shoulders.

When times are tough, this position just feels lonely. It's a place where no one can really tell me what to do. For example, I've been wrestling with a big leadership decision over the last couple of months. People's futures are at stake. I realize that I hold in the palm of my hand people's livelihood and their future careers. I have had to fire people through the years, and that feels very lonely. It is especially painful when you have to fire people you hired and believed in. In those times I think about how that person will make his or her mortgage payment and how the spouse will react when he or she comes home with the bad news.

In this current crisis I cried out to God and said, "Please just send someone to tell me what to do." I have a lot of advisers who think they know the right decision, but they don't all agree with each other. Sometimes those who advise you have their own not-so-hidden agendas. And when it comes right down to this particular decision, only I can make it. Making tough decisions is a lonely chore, and being criticized by people who don't understand the full story is lonely. But that's the job.

> THERE IS A LEVEL OF TRANSPARENCY IN A SAFE FRIENDSHIP THAT CANNOT HAPPEN AT THE WORKPLACE.

We all need confidants who are not colleagues. There is a level of transparency in a safe friendship that cannot happen at the workplace. No matter how much community we try to have, I am still an authority over others. So I have found precious friendships through the years with people outside of my work.

Just last week I went to California to spend a day with my friend Craig. We've been friends for over thirty years, and there's nothing I wouldn't tell Craig. We had an awesome day together, unburdening our hearts about our struggles and challenges. We sat at a restaurant on the beach and just talked for hours. It was a day of pure therapy for me, and I feel fortunate to have such a friend.

I do believe that your spouse is not enough. Some leaders dump way too much on their spouses and experience negative effects. I do share a lot with Donna, but I don't want her to be my dumping ground. Since she does not work with me, she can develop a skewed perspective. She can become bitter against people I work with if I complain to her about them. I just might forget to tell her when it's all resolved, and she is still angry long after I have moved on! Complaining to someone who doesn't have a dog in the fight is a totally different dynamic. So make sure you have a Craig.

CONFIDE IN THOSE ABOVE YOU — ONLY GRIPE UPSTREAM

Do your whining in the right place, and complain to those upstream. Let me illustrate with a great movie clip. There is a great scene in the movie *Saving Private Ryan* that I love to show when I teach on this point. This movie is Steven Spielberg's grisly, realistic account of a squad of D-day survivors sent behind enemy lines on a mission to rescue the last living son of a devastated Iowa family. The goal of this particular squad is to save young Private Ryan and bring him home to his mother. Having previously experienced action in Italy and North Africa, the close-knit squad sets off through areas crawling with Nazis. After they lose one man in a skirmish at a bombed village, some in the group begin to question the logic of losing more lives to save a single soldier. Tom Hanks gives an amazing performance as the squad's tormented leader, Captain Miller.

In one scene, they are walking through the French countryside, openly sharing their doubts about the mission, and morale is at an all-time low:

Jackson (Barry Pepper): Sir, I have an opinion on this matter.

Miller (Tom Hanks): Well, by all means, share it with the squad.

Jackson: Well, from my way of thinking, sir, this entire mission is a serious misallocation of valuable military resources.... It seems to me, sir, that God gave me a special gift, made me a fine instrument of warfare.

Miller: Reiben, pay attention. Now, this is the way to gripe....

Jackson goes on and gripes about the war for a few more seconds.

Reiben (Edward Burns): That's brilliant, [Jackson]. Hey, so, Captain, what about you? I mean, you don't gripe at all?

Miller looks at Reiben, shocked.

Miller: I don't gripe to *you*, Reiben. I'm a captain. There's a chain of command. Gripes go up, not down. Always up. You gripe to me; I gripe to my superior officer.... I don't gripe to you. I don't gripe in front of you. You should know that as a Ranger.

For me, griping upstream would include my board and, of course, God. I am so thankful for a board chairman who listens and supports me so well in this way. What happens if we gripe too much to those who are under our leadership? They might just lose confidence in us and become overly discouraged themselves. There is a difference between me showing vulnerability in leadership and pouring out my heart about the situations that frustrate me the most. Gripe your discouragements to your outside confidants, to your boss, to your board, and especially to God.

FINALLY, REMEMBER AND TAKE COURAGE FROM THOSE WHO BELIEVE IN YOU

When I feel down and think the world is against me, I like to remember the people who believe in me. They are sort of like my personal secret fan club. Some of them are alive, and others have gone on to be with Jesus. I have an encouragement file that I've kept for years. It is a folder (and also a subfolder in my email) labeled "encouragement." As I wrote these words, I got out the folder and started reading through the letters, notes, and scribbles that people have sent me through the years. It gave me a boost to realize that, yes, there are quite a few people who appreciate what I do and appreciate me!

To take this idea to the next level, I did something kind of crazy a couple of years ago. In my office in Colorado I bought a small bulletin board that is quite unusual. I have hung it in an out-of-the-way place that I can see from my desk, but visitors would never know it is there. It's one foot wide and two and a half feet tall—just right for the end of my bookcase. I found photos of all my mentors who invested personally in my life as a leader. Some photos go back thirty-five years. I call it my *Mentors Wall*. Each of these men and women encouraged me along my journey. They believe in Hans. I look at those pictures that say to me every day, "Remember what you learned from our example, and finish strong—make us proud." I wish I could find a photo of Moses, too. My mentors keep me going when the going gets really rough.

WE ALL NEED ENCOURAGEMENT

My daughter, Cambria, has always told me that I intimidate her friends: "Dad, you scare them. You are so tall and confident and sure of yourself." Just this week, one of my staff members was shocked when I revealed that I suffer from great feelings of inadequacy. But what people don't realize is that I need just as much encouragement as the most timid and shy person. Confident people need compliments too. I think people don't take the time to compliment or encourage their leaders because they assume there is some secret sauce of positive energy that keeps us pumped up. Well, we all need it just as much. *I know that I do.* It reminds me of these words from Phyllis Theroux:

> One of the commodities in life that most people can't get enough of is compliments. The ego is never so intact that one can't find a hole in which to plug a little praise. But compliments, by their very nature, are highly biodegradable and tend to dissolve hours or days after we receive them—which is why we can always use another.[4]

10

LEADERSHIP COMMANDMENT #10: THOU SHALT KEEP THINE EYES ON THE PRIZE

By faith Moses, when he had grown up, refused to be known as the son of Pharaoh's daughter. He chose to be mistreated along with the people of God rather than to enjoy the pleasures of sin for a short time. He regarded disgrace for the sake of Christ as of greater value than the treasures of Egypt, because he was looking ahead to his reward. (Heb. 11:24–26)

Big Idea: Motivation to lead should come from a calling higher than just serving people or making a living. The drive to keep going comes when we serve our values, we serve our God, and we serve our passion, vision, and calling. We do not simply work for the organization or people who hired us.

I love being the son of Alfred Finzel. Last week I had the chance to return to his hometown of Leipzig, Germany, with my youngest son, Andrew. I had the joy of showing Andrew where his grandpa studied metallurgy and machining at the University of Leipzig.

Andrew never met my dad, because he died before Andrew was born. But my children all know that their grandfather had a special place in the history of the US space program, and it started for my dad at this university in Germany during World War II. He was drafted into the German war effort; sent to work on V1 and V2 missiles, where he worked for the famous scientist Wernher von Braun; and then brought to America to help the US space program. America was good to my parents. They received a warm welcome and citizenship, and my father had a great career working for NASA in Alabama. As I said in the beginning of this book, you don't have to be a rocket scientist to be the proud son of one.

My father was hugely disappointed when I shifted my entire life to follow Christ. It was not Christ he was upset with so much as my career change. I went overboard in his mind. I left the University of Alabama and pursued ministry studies at Columbia International University, which upset both of my parents. I remember them saying to me in those years, "You could be so successful. Why are you throwing your life away with this religious stuff?" In their minds I was going to a monastery and putting on a white collar. Their view of success was very different from my own. My mother was so upset about my going to Columbia, she didn't even bother attending my college graduation.

After college I decided to go to seminary, and that made matters worse. Finally, after graduate school, Donna and I moved overseas with

WorldVenture—a nonprofit ministry—and lived on donations. That was as bad as it could get for my parents—"If you have a family, how will you support them?" they asked. In terms of their dreams for me, their son was a failure. I had no chance for success in their minds. They did not have the eyes to see Matthew 6:33: "But seek first his kingdom and his righteousness, and all these things will be given to you as well."

That was the price I had to pay for following my calling. It hurt, but I had to follow my heart. The good news is "the rest of the story." While both of my parents are no longer living, my relationship with my father ended on a very positive, encouraging note in 1984. Sadly, he contracted lung cancer that year and was given just a few months to live. Interesting how different life looks when you face eternity. The last time I talked to my dad, I asked him to go out for coffee so we could talk. I told him how much I loved him and how proud I was to be his son. What he said back to me that day in that restaurant in Indianapolis has been huge for me ever since. A man's last words are lasting words. He said, "Son, I was disappointed with your career choice in the early years. I'm sorry. *I now know that what you chose to do with your life is more important than anything I ever accomplished.* You have decided to make the world a better place and truly help people." I could not believe his words of affirmation. And he had helped put a man on the moon! You have no idea how much closure that brought to me. He finally "got" what Donna and I were doing with the calling on our lives. He died at the end of 1984 a man at peace with God. In those last months, he believed in the Jesus I have followed all my adult life.

Some pay a dear price to follow their calling. Much more than I have. As I was writing this final chapter, terrible news came in from Kabul, Afghanistan, about ten aid workers who were gunned down and murdered in cold blood. I thought how much their lives spoke to this issue of following a higher calling. It was because of their calling that they were executed. The aid workers had a deep commitment to Afghanistan and knew the risks associated with humanitarian work there, friends and families of the victims said. The aid workers were killed by gunmen in Badakhshan, a remote northeastern region of the country. Among the dead were six Americans, two Afghans, a Briton, and a German. Tom Little was among a small number of Americans who had been in Afghanistan for decades, working with international aid agencies and other nongovernmental organizations. These men and women were dedicated to making life better for the Afghan people: providing clean water, decent health care. Dr. Karen Woo from Great Britain had given up a safe job in London working as a doctor in order to help the poor and needy in Afghanistan. It was reported that gunmen stopped the workers on the road, took their belongings, and shot them one by one. The Taliban claimed responsibility for the attack. As the news reports have come in, time and again reporters were told that these ten were following a calling to do good in this war-torn country. I know from direct accounts that these were people with a strong faith in God that drove their passion. It reminds me of that great quote from Tertullian: "The blood of the martyrs is the seed of the church."

Why do people put up with the tough side of leadership and the burdens that come with the job? Why do they risk all for their passion? They follow a calling. I work with great people scattered in tough places all over the world, subjecting themselves to harsh circumstances and stress galore. Why do they do it? Why not just stay on the shores of America and enjoy the good life? The drive to keep going comes because they follow their passion, vision, and calling. People who change the world do not simply work for the organization or people who hired them.

> **FOLLOW THE MOST COMPELLING OF MANY OPTIONS AT ANY COST.**

I have a simple definition of calling that I came up with years ago. It's a simple phrase, but in my mind it covers the entire issue: "Follow the most compelling of many options at any cost."

CALLING

FOLLOW THE MOST COMPELLING

What drives you? What is your biggest dream about what you would like to do? If there were no obstacles, what would you like to get involved with? How would you like to leave an impact with your life?

OF MANY OPTIONS

There are many great things you can do with your life. Instead of worrying about finding the center of God's bull's-eye for you, His without question perfect plan for your life, seek to pursue the option that draws you the most. I have seen that there is rarely one perfect thing to do with your life—there are many choices. And I believe that when we look back in the rearview mirror, we will find that God would have been pleased with a number of options we might have chosen. Some get paralyzed into doing nothing because they are too worried about missing the perfect mark. A simple principle of finding God's plan for your life is to *keep moving!*

AT ANY COST

This is where most people stumble and settle for less than the best. Paying the price can include both *that which you have to give up* as well as *that which you have to experience*. You might be called away from comfort toward a life of hardship and sacrifice. I think that's what Jesus had in mind when He told us that we need to take up our crosses daily in order to follow Him fully. Pursuing a calling will require sacrifice in most cases.

A good friend asked me the other night, "Why didn't you leave your position during the dark days of your discouragement? Why do you put up with some of that stuff? You had lots of other options." It's because of my call. God called me to do the work I am doing, and He didn't release me to quit until just recently. To me, a call is not about an audible voice or some other direct communication from God. It's more subjective and subtle. It is a drive to do something that you cannot get out of your heart. This drive gets under your skin, and you become obsessed with it. The call could be a quiet whisper from God, or it might just well up in your heart over a period of time. For my friend Craig Weaver, it happened when I took him on a vision trip to China—and his heart melted with the needs and the opportunity.

Many people find their calling when they see human misery in other lands. Blake Mycoskie came home from a mission trip where he had worked with poor kids in South America, and he founded Toms Shoes. Like it says on the company website, Toms.com, "With every pair you purchase, TOMS will give a pair of new shoes to a child in need. One for one." What a great illustration of following a call. To follow your calling is to rise above mediocrity and make a difference in the world with your life.

The unfolding story of any leader's journey, like that of Moses, should be about making such a big difference that it makes the sacrifice worth it. Leaders make things happen. History is the story of leaders, good and bad, who have shaped the world as we know it in one way or another. The thing I enjoy the most about my own leadership journey is when God uses me to resolve big challenges. I like fixing things that are broken, and I rise to a large challenge. I have always been of the opinion that *need constitutes call*—so find a need, and fill it.

> TO FOLLOW YOUR CALLING IS TO RISE ABOVE MEDIOCRITY AND MAKE A DIFFERENCE IN THE WORLD WITH YOUR LIFE.

Sometimes when I attend funerals, I can't help but ponder what people will say about me when my time comes. For Moses, his funeral was the celebration of a life well lived. We know what people said about Moses when he died, because we know his story and we know he finished well. What an epitaph! Moses died at 120 years of age; his eyes were still clear, and the Bible says he was as strong as ever:

> Since then, no prophet has risen in Israel like
> Moses, whom the LORD knew face to face, who did
> all those miraculous signs and wonders the LORD

sent him to do in Egypt—to Pharaoh and to all his
officials and to his whole land. For no one has ever
shown the mighty power or performed the awesome deeds that Moses did in the sight of all Israel.
(Deut. 34:10–12)

John Carver, who specializes in helping nonprofits with board
governance, has a great statement about the reason an organization
exists. His comment speaks directly to this issue of cause: "The only
justifiable reason for organizational existence is the production of
worthwhile results."[1]

Motivation to lead must be drawn from a great cause. *Who* do
we serve, and *what* crying need are we trying to solve? This is what
keeps us going in the tough times. We live in tough times, but the
right leader with the right calling can change the world. Leaders
fill a need in organizations for direction, deliverance, rescue, and
more. For Moses, the need that he filled is laid out clearly in the
beginning of the book of Exodus in the midst of the description of
his birth. His birth story makes clear the need for which God was
already grooming him to resolve. God came up with a rescue plan:

During that long period, the king of Egypt died.
The Israelites groaned in their slavery and cried
out, and their cry for help because of their slavery
went up to God. God heard their groaning and
he remembered his covenant with Abraham, with
Isaac and with Jacob. *So God looked on the Israelites
and was concerned about them.* (Ex. 2:23–25)

That was the need, and God called Moses to fill it. It is one of the great, dramatic stories of the Bible. I love that it says, "God looked on the Israelites and was concerned about them" (v. 25). He sees our plight, and it concerns Him. However, His timing and our preferred timing are not usually on the same schedule. But I find it interesting that the text mentions that God looked down on the Israelites and was concerned about them. And He mobilized Moses as the leader to fix the problem. But it would be another forty years before deliverance would come, because it would come through a leader who was not yet ready. Forty years after the call of Moses at the burning bush, he arrived to help the people. What is the leadership lesson here? When the right leader is prepared, then God can use him or her for His purposes. Our job is to prepare; His job is to use us where and when He needs us.

EYES FIXED ON OUR LEADER

For Christ followers, keeping our eyes on the prize has a lot to do with keeping our eyes on Jesus. This focus helps us when we want to bail. I had to remind my daughter, Cambria, about this not long ago during some discouraging days on her mission team. She works with Youth With A Mission and is having a great impact working with marginalized kids around the world. As she has traveled the world with a team of young female adults, they have experienced major drama from time to time. Frankly, some of the other team members have been mean and divisive. I'm sure my daughter did her fair share of griping as part of a team that lives together, travels together, and works together. Close quarters can bring out the worst in us at times. I reminded her that Christians will let her down, but Jesus never will. I think that this is exactly what the writer of Hebrews had in mind. When I wrote Cambria with my fatherly advice, I included the following verse handwritten on a yellow pad for emphasis. It's always helped me keep my eyes on God, not on people:

> Therefore, since we are surrounded by such a great cloud of witnesses, let us throw off everything that hinders and the sin that so easily entangles, and let us run with perseverance the race marked out for us. *Let us fix our eyes on Jesus, the author and perfecter of our faith*, who for the joy set before him endured the cross, scorning its shame, and sat down at the right hand of the throne of God. *Consider him who endured such opposition from sinful men, so that you will not grow weary and lose heart.* (Heb. 12:1–3)

WE ALL HAVE THE CHOICE

Effective leadership is about pursuing a higher purpose, not about pleasing people. We who are Christ followers must listen to the voice of God, and He calls us to pursue a higher purpose in life. One of the voices that inspired my passion over the years recently died and went on to his reward. On many occasions I've been inspired to keep pushing for the prize by the voice of Jim Rohn. I never heard him in person, but I have devoured many of his audio lectures. Here's a small selection that matches up perfectly with my definition of the call of God on our lives:

> Each of us has two distinct choices to make about what we will do with our lives. The first choice we can make is to be less than we have the capacity to be. To earn less. To have less. To read less and think less. To try less and discipline ourselves less. These are the choices that lead to an empty life. These are the choices that, once made, lead to a life of constant apprehension instead of a life of wondrous anticipation.
>
> And the second choice? To do it all! To become all that we can possibly be. To read every book that we possibly can. To earn as much as we possibly can. To give and share as much as we possibly can. To strive and produce and accomplish as much as we possibly can. All of us have the choice.[2]

Somehow through the wilderness and all the whining, Moses kept God in mind. That has to be one of the big reasons he did not quit. He chose to stay in the game. When I think of *keeping our eyes on the prize,* I think of a little sentence in Matthew 25: "His master replied, 'Well done, good and faithful servant! You have been faithful with a few things; I will put you in charge of many things. Come and share your master's happiness!'" (v. 21).

I want to spend eternity sharing in the Master's happiness. How cool does that sound?

FINAL WORD: "ESTABLISH THE WORK OF OUR HANDS"

I have enjoyed my journey with Moses, and I hope you have too. I think you will agree that his life was epic and instructive on so many levels. No wonder he remains such a popular and well-known figure today. I never thought about putting these lessons into a book until the leadership storms passed and I realized how much I learned from him. When I see him someday, I will thank him for helping rescue me during the stormy middle of my leadership life. I envision a long line of people wanting to greet him in heaven, but I am willing to wait.

If you want to read the entire account of his life, you can do so through the passages that I listed in the introduction of this book. It is best to read the direct words of the Bible if you want to get to the heart of the story. Charles Swindoll wrote a great practical and devotional book about Moses that I would commend to you: *Moses: A Man of Selfless Dedication,* volume 4 in the Great Lives from God's Word series.

Moses deserves the last word. I choose to end this book with his special prayer from the book of Psalms. He only wrote one that we know of: Psalm 90. I highly suggest you read the whole thing—it's not long. Do so in a quiet place where you can pray the words to God. And be sure to listen to God's quiet whispers back to you.

Psalm 90 is filled with wisdom and honesty and thankfulness for a life well lived. It is actually titled in the Scriptures: "*A prayer of Moses the man of God.*" If any character in the Bible deserves that label, it is Moses. I love the end of this psalm in verse 17, which expresses so well the bottom line of what we all want as leaders: "May the favor of the Lord our God rest upon us; establish the work of our hands for us—yes, establish the work of our hands."

> Lord, you have been our dwelling place
> > throughout all generations.
> Before the mountains were born
> > or you brought forth the earth and the world,
> > from everlasting to everlasting you are God.
>
> You turn men back to dust,
> > saying, "Return to dust, O sons of men."
> For a thousand years in your sight
> > are like a day that has just gone by,
> > or like a watch in the night....
>
> Teach us to number our days aright,
> > that we may gain a heart of wisdom....
>
> May the favor of the Lord our God rest upon us;
> > establish the work of our hands for us—
> > yes, establish the work of our hands. (Ps. 90:1–4, 12, 17)

NOTES

PREFACE

1. *The Free Dictionary,* s.v. "diligence," accessed September 19, 2011,
www.thefreedictionary.com/diligence.
2. Dean R. Hoge and Jacqueline E. Wenger, *Pastors in Transition* (Grand Rapids:
Eerdmans, 2005), 37.
3. Matthew Stewart, *The Management Myth* (New York: W. W. Norton &
Company, 2009), 5.
4. Ibid., 13.

INTRODUCTION TO MOSES

1. *The Free Dictionary,* s.v. "epic," accessed September 19, 2011,
www.thefreedictionary.com/epic.

2. Cathy Lynn Grossman, "Is Moses the Man Who Shaped America?" *USA Today,*
   October 21, 2009, www.usatoday.com/news/religion/2009-10-20-moses-
   america_N.htm.

3. D. L. Moody, quoted in Charles Swindoll, *Moses: A Man of Selfless Dedication*
   (Nashville: Thomas Nelson, 1999), 20.

1. LEADERSHIP COMMANDMENT #1: THOU SHALT CLING TO THE VISION

1. James Kouzes and Barry Posner, *The Leadership Challenge* (San Francisco: Jossey-
   Bass, 1987), 32.

2. Stephen Covey, *The 7 Habits of Highly Effective People* (New York: Fireside,
   1990), 101.

3. Ibid.

4. Burt Nanus, *Visionary Leadership* (San Francisco: Jossey-Bass, 1992), 8, 16.

5. Ibid., 28–29.

6. Bill Hybels, *Axiom* (Grand Rapids: Zondervan, 2008), 30.

2. LEADERSHIP COMMANDMENT #2: THOU SHALT NOT SERVE THINE OWN EGO

1. Rick Warren, *The Purpose Driven Life* (Grand Rapids: Zondervan, 2002), 21.

3. Leadership Commandment #3: Thou Shalt Practice Servant Leadership

1. Herb Kelleher, "A Culture of Commitment," *Leader to Leader* 4 (1997): 20 –24, www.leadertoleader.org/knowledgecenter/journal.aspx?ArticleID=143.
2. Timothy Laniak, *While Shepherds Watch Their Flocks* (Matthews, NC: ShepherdLeader Publications, 2007), 29.

4. Leadership Commandment #4: Thou Shalt Be Opposed, Resisted, and Misunderstood

1. Jim Collins, *Good to Great* (New York: HarperCollins, 2001), 13.
2. *The Free Dictionary,* s.v. "grumble," accessed September 19, 2011, www.thefreedictionary.com/grumble.
3. *Oxford Dictionaries,* s.v. "insolent," accessed September 19, 2011, http://oxforddictionaries.com/definition/insolent?region=us.
4. *Wikipedia,* s.v. "360-degree feedback," last modified April 4, 2011, http://en.wikipedia.org/wiki/360-degree_feedback.
5. Ken Williams, lecture handout, October 1, 1996.
6. Abraham Lincoln, quoted in Francis Carpenter, *Six Months at the White House with Abraham Lincoln* (New York: Hurd and Houghton, 1866), 258.

5. Leadership Commandment #5: Thou Shalt Have a Life

1. Matthew Stewart, *The Management Myth* (New York: W. W. Norton & Company, 2009), 5.
2. Lou Cannon, *President Reagan* (New York: PublicAffairs, 2000), 154.
3. "Vacation Deprivation Key Statistic," Expedia.com, www.expedia.com/daily/ promos/vacations/vacation_deprivation/.
4. "Expedia.com—2009 International Vacation Deprivation™ Survey Results," Expedia.com, 2009, http://media.expedia.com/media/content/expus/graphics/ promos/vacations/Expedia_International_Vacation_Deprivation_Survey_2009. pdf, 2.
5. Ibid., 7.

6. Leadership Commandment #6: Thou Shalt Sweat the Small Stuff

1. *Dictionary.com Unabridged,* s.v. "integrity," http://dictionary.reference.com/ browse/integrity.
2. John C. Maxwell, author, speaker, and founder INJOY Stewardship Services and EQUIP, email to the author, September 2007. Used with permission.
3. The Associated Press and Reuters, "HP's CEO Hurd Quits after Sexual-Harassment Probe," *MSNBC.com,* August 7, 2010, www.msnbc.msn.com/ id/38597967/ns/business-us_business/t/hps-ceo-hurd-quits-after-sexual-harassment-probe/#.TkrtMoXAY2Q.

8. Leadership Commandment #8: Thou Shalt Lead to Leave

1. Max Lucado, *He Still Moves Stones* (Nashville: Thomas Nelson, 1993), 67.
2. Jerry Rankin, email to the author, September 2007. Used with permission.

9. Leadership Commandment #9: Thou Shalt Never Give Up

1. Quotes taken from Bluefish TV, *Famous Failures,* www.bluefishtv.com/Store/ Downloadable_Video_Illustrations/1378/Famous_Failures__Lesson_Available_ Used with permission.
2. Peter Pendell, email to the author, July 12, 2011. Used with permission.
3. "About *StrengthsFinder 2.0,*" Strengths, http://strengths.gallup.com/110440/ About-StrengthsFinder-2.aspx.
4. Phyllis Theroux, *Parents,* quoted in *Reader's Digest* 132 (1988): 218.

10. Leadership Commandment #10: Thou Shalt Keep Thine Eyes on the Prize

1. John Carver, *Boards That Make a Difference* (San Francisco: Jossey-Bass, 2006), 79.
2. Jim Rohn, *Leading an Inspired Life* (Niles, IL: Nightingale-Conant, 1996), page number unknown.

ACKNOWLEDGMENTS

Thanks to my dear wife, Donna, for standing by my side through all the ups and downs of my leadership journey. Without her I would have bailed long ago. She is my most trusted adviser.

My editors, Alex Field and Caitlyn York, did an amazing job with the raw ingredients I handed them in cooking up a great presentation of my words and thoughts.

For over twenty-five years David C Cook has been a great publisher to work with, and I continue to enjoy the relationship.

To those I lead, I appreciate your grace and mercy as I stumble along and try to get better.

ABOUT THE AUTHOR

The son of a rocket scientist, Hans Finzel had his sights set high early in life. Hans is a first-generation American whose parents moved from Germany to Alabama just before his birth. His father, Alfred Finzel, was one of over a hundred German scientists brought to America by the US Army at the end of World War II with their leader Dr. Wernher von Braun to "launch" the US space program.

Hans and his wife, Donna, joined WorldVenture in 1980 and have had a career of leadership spanning over three decades with this ministry. Before moving to headquarters, they spent the decade of the 1980s living in Vienna, Austria, as field staff with WorldVenture. During that exciting decade, they devoted themselves to ministry throughout Eastern Europe, training pastors and leaders behind the Iron Curtain in a Biblical Education by Extension ministry. Hans was in Berlin in November 1989 to witness the fall of the wall.

Hans served as the president and CEO of WorldVenture for twenty years. WorldVenture's focus is evangelism, compassion, church planting, and leadership development ministries with an international workforce of over six hundred staff. Under his leadership, the mission experienced great expansion of ministry from twenty-nine to over seventy countries.

Hans is a successful author, teacher, and leader among leaders. He has trained leaders internationally on five continents. He has authored seven books, including his popular *The Top Ten Mistakes Leaders Make* (David C Cook). Hans has extensive experience in public speaking, consulting, and seminar facilitation, and he also teaches leadership as adjunct faculty at various colleges and graduate schools in the United States and internationally. Hans holds a bachelor's degree (BA) from Columbia International University, a master's degree (ThM) from Dallas Theological Seminary, and a doctorate in leadership (DMiss) from Fuller School of Intercultural Studies. Hans and Donna have four children and make their home in Colorado.

Hans can be reached to answer your leadership questions or for resources, speaking, teaching, or consulting services at www.hansfinzel.com.

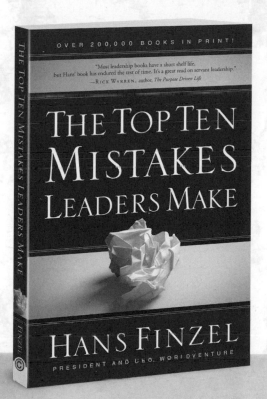